PRAISE FOR *SUBLIME UNION*

"Mercedes Kirkel is one of the clearest channels of Mary Magdalene known to humankind. Her material seems to access the same aspect of Magdalene as found in the original Gospel of Mary Magdalene—one of the "lost" books of the Bible. *Sublime Union* is an extraordinary and thorough work, covering everything from metaphysics to honoring emotions, life in the ancient Holy Land, and how to experience sacred sexuality in our lives and relationships. The reader is taken through practical exercises to open the chakras, open the heart, and open to the union of the Divine Feminine and Masculine—inside and out."

—Michael Mirdad, author of *An Introduction to Tantra and Sacred Sexuality* and *Creating Fulfilling Relationships*

"*Sublime Union* is the book we've all been waiting for. I highly recommend this thrilling read."

—Christiane Northrup, MD, author of *Women's Bodies, Women's Wisdom*

"Beautifully written and juicy, to put it mildly, *Sublime Union* is a landmark book. In this poignant, courageously vulnerable love story, Kirkel opens up her intimate dance and erotic journey with her partner, allowing the reader to feel his or her own depths while riding a wild wave of real transformation. Woven throughout is a grounded and finely illustrated manual for sexual practice in the realms of communication, energy exchange, and more. I recommend this book highly!"

—Saniel Bonder, author of *Healing the Spirit/Matter Split* and *While Jesus Weeps*

"Awakened sexuality is an opening to the Divine. I applaud your courage for sharing your sacred sex life with the world in order to teach this, so people will have an opportunity to have a much more fulfilling and spiritual relationship."

—Joanna Prentis, coauthor of *Power of the Magdalene* and *The Magdalene Version*

"A multifaceted jewel of a book that shimmers with light and love. Candid and intriguing personal transformation is delicately interwoven with profound wisdom and amplified by valuable energy-raising practices. Compelling and convincing."

—Diana Richardson, author of *The Heart of Tantric Sex* and *Slow Sex*

"Passionate, powerful, and, best of all, extremely practical, *Sublime Union* can help couples open to the sacredness of sex and love, and heal their bodies, minds, and souls."

—Stephanie Riseley, author of *Love From Both Sides*

"For those who choose sacred sexuality as a path to touch enlightenment and embrace sublime union, Mary Magdalene and Mercedes Kirkel offer clear and timely guidance pointing the way."

—Claire Heartsong, author of *Anna, Grandmother of Jesus*

"The words within *Sublime Union* flow like exquisite poetry, wrapping around you like a cloak from the Divine Mother. This book is a 'must read' for all those on the Magdalene path."

—Anaiya Sophia, author of *Sacred Sexual Union* and *The Rose Knight*

"A great manual for creating sacred, healthy, and loving relationships, and a perfect prelude to attracting just the right partner in one's life."

—Elizabeth Wright, author of *I & Eye*

"*Sublime Union* is a giant leap forward in assisting humanity to overcome taboos and negativity about human sexuality."

—Ronna Herman, author of *Revealed Cosmic Truths for Ascending Humanity*

"A divine love story . . . where passion and the sacred are one."

—Caroline Muir, author of *Tantra Goddess*

"These teachings bring illumination to the sacredness of sex for all of us—integrating passion, pleasure, and love in a sacred way."

—Diane Riley, coauthor of *Tantric Secrets for Men*, author of *Sexy and Sacred*

SUBLIME UNION

A Woman's Sexual Odyssey
Guided by Mary Magdalene

BOOK TWO OF THE MAGDALENE TEACHINGS

Mercedes Kirkel

INTO THE HEART
Creations

SANTA FE, NEW MEXICO

Published by INTO THE HEART CREATIONS
PO Box 32742, Santa Fe, NM 87594 • www.intotheheart.org

Book design and graphics by Angela Werneke

Cover art by Aesha Kennedy
with digital enhancements by Teri Yarbrow and Max Almy

Illustrations by Rebecca Farr

First edition

Printed in the United States of America

Publisher's Cataloging-in-Publication Data

Kirkel, Mercedes.

Sublime union : a woman's sexual odyssey guided by Mary Magdalene / Mercedes Kirkel. — 1st ed. — Santa Fe, N.M. : Into the Heart Creations, c2014.

p. ; cm.
(The Magdalene teachings ; book 2)
ISBN: 978-0-9840029-1-7

Includes bibliographical references.

Summary: Follow Mary Magdalene on a profound journey into the world of sacred sexuality. Sublime Union presents Mary Magdalene's instruction (given to author Mercedes Kirkel) on the techniques of sacred sexuality. Mary describes in detail the sexual practices she learned through the temple of Isis, including the advanced form she engaged with Yeshua (Jesus). Woven together with these communications is Kirkel's stirring story of applying Mary's teaching with her partner. Both a sacred sexuality manual and erotic memoir, Sublime Union brings the "master awakening the student" genre into the bedroom. A fascinating narrative that will leave you changed! —Publisher.

1. Mary Magdalene, Saint—Sexual behavior. 2. Goddess religion. 3. Sex—Religious aspects. 4. Sex—Religious aspects—Tantrism. 5. Sex instruction. 6. Sexual exercises. 7. Sex customs. 8. Jesus Christ—New Age movement interpretations. 9. Jesus Christ—Family. 10. Isis (Egyptian deity)—Sexual behavior. 11. Spirit writings. 12. Channeling (Spiritualism) 13. Spiritual biography. 14. Kirkel, Mercedes—Sexual behavior. I. Mary Magdalene, Saint (Spirit) II. Title. III. Series: Magdalene teaching ; book 2.

BS2485 .K57 2012
226/.092--dc23   1407

1 3 5 7 9 10 8 6 4 2

To Mary Magdalene,
with deepest gratitude
for her love and wisdom

Acknowledgments

MY FIRST AND DEEPEST THANKS go to Mary Magdalene. I'm profoundly grateful for her immense love, compassion, and wisdom, which she has demonstrated to me without fail on every occasion in which I've had contact with her. I'm moved beyond words for the caring she has for human beings at this time and how much she wants to help us. And I'm continually inspired by her modeling of an awakened, powerful woman who's completely in love with the Divene Masculine and who lives the glorious Masculine-Feminine union—both within herself and in partnership with another.

I'm exceedingly thankful to all my friends who have supported, encouraged, and nurtured me throughout the process of creating this book. My thanks to my mother, father, stepmother, and daughter; to Richard, Madeleine, Tom, Angela, Lawrence, David, Karina, Stephan, and so many others. Thank you all for being there for me, in countless ways.

More thanks, to all the tremendously gifted, highly professional people who've made this book so much stronger: Aesha Kennedy for the exquisite painting you created for the cover of the book; Teri Yarbrow and Max Almy for your digital magic on the cover image; Rebecca Farr for your illustrations that perfectly capture the various descriptions; Angela Werneke for your marvelous aesthetic abilities in pulling all the artwork and text together in a consummate design, both on the cover and interior—as well as guiding me with your sage counsel and holding my hand every step of the way; Ellen Kleiner for your excellent editing; and Barbara Doern Drew for your careful proofing. A special thanks to the early readers, who reassured me that this was a great book: Kate Marks, Susan Lockary, Hope Kiah, Ron Tobin, Trey Hammond, and Joanna Prentis.

To all the people who contributed to my fundraising campaign for producing this book, please know that you not only supported the publication of this book financially. You also gave me much-needed encouragement and staying power when I was feeling overwhelmed and alone in the process. I strongly believe that Mary wanted this book to be produced by a group effort, and your donations were a huge part of that. To Tamara (Tammy) Braswell, Noel Onion, Martina Sand, Teresa Carty, Michelle Krumland, Aida Sanchez, Tom Marks, David Spinney, and Brad Dole, please accept my special thanks for your very generous contributions.

Finally, I wish to thank all the men who have loved me in so many ways throughout my life, beginning with my father and including my partners through the various periods of my journey. I'm blessed to have been so incredibly loved by such great and beautiful men. And most especially, I'm grateful beyond words to "Tony," who lived this miraculous story with me and was so instrumental in bringing it to fruition. I thank you from the fullness of my heart.

Why else do we make love
if not to seek the original unity?

—Burl Hall
Sophia's Web: Reclaiming Wholeness in a Divided World

Contents

PART II ~ INTERMEDIATE PRACTICES

PART III ~ ADVANCED PRACTICES

Illustrations

Mary Magdalene and Her Current Mission

MARY MAGDALENE is known to many as a woman who traveled with Jesus as one of his primary followers. Beyond that simple statement, there is great controversy over her identity. For centuries, she was viewed as a prostitute and repentant sinner. Yet in 1969 the Catholic Church declared that such a conclusion was unfounded and made her a saint. *The Da Vinci Code* by Dan Brown, a book published in 2003, helped popularize the idea that Mary Magdalene was Jesus's wife and that they had children together. Numerous people go even further and view Mary Magdalene as Jesus's twin flame or soul companion, and many see her as a spiritual icon of Divine Feminine empowerment, wisdom, and leadership.

I have had the great honor of channeling a being who identifies herself as Mary Magdalene. She first initiated contact with me in 2010 through communications in which she described herself as Jesus's sacred partner. Those communications were meticulously recorded in book one of The Magdalene Teachings, entitled *Mary Magdalene Beckons: Join the River of Love*:

> In truth, I was Yeshua's sacred partner.[1] We were equals, as holy man and woman, holy husband and wife. Just as there is no separation within our Mother-Father God—both aspects are equal and yet truly beyond equality, simply two faces of the Divine Being—so were Yeshua and I.[2] We loved each other completely and still do. We saw each other as the divine self. We both were prepared for our meeting and relationship with each other, through the many schools and traditions of our times. My training was primarily through the Egyptian temple of Isis, where I was trained as a high priestess. There were

many forms of being a priestess in this lineage. Many involved healing and blessing work. I was trained in the highest arts of serving the Divine through what was called Sacred Relationship. This was a school, or stream, within the temple, a very high one. . . .

[W]e were in Sacred Relationship with each other, and this included sacred sexual relationship. We were both prepared for this through the training we received individually through sacred traditions, especially the Egyptian and Indian sacred paths. We engaged in lovemaking as a process of transforming our bodies into light and love, in service to our destinies. And we were deeply in love with each other. We lived this love through all aspects of our lives, and both of us were dedicated to the work that Yeshua was the leader for.

Today, as two thousand years ago, we are dedicated to supporting all humans in this process of upliftment and growth in God's love and light. The form has evolved, but the calling and core is the same. I am devoted to being a kind of midwife at this time of the next phase of this Grand Plan, and thus I come to you with my messages in support of that.[3]

Sublime Union tells the story of a five-month period of time in 2012, when Mary Magdalene delivered a second series of messages to me. Unlike her earlier communications, these were directed specifically to me and pertained to my spiritual journey. Yet contained within them was invaluable wisdom and guidance in the ways of sacred sexuality that clearly applied to others as well. From the start, I sensed that Mary was using me as a vehicle for bringing her instruction to light. And I was happy to serve her in this way, believing it would be a tremendous boon to others.

Right away I began recording the guidance I received from her and, soon thereafter, the implementing of it in my relationship with my partner. Throughout that time of receiving and living Mary's teaching, I experienced everything that occurred in my life as a seamless whole. Nothing seemed coincidental or extraneous. It was all her great gift and blessing, given not just for my partner and myself but for all who might be touched by our experiences.

The messages from Mary were most often given to me during my morning meditation. Knowing she was likely to communicate with me, I would have my laptop nearby. Then, after completing my daily practice, I would open my computer, place my fingers on the keyboard, and close my eyes. Almost immediately I would perceive Mary's characteristic presence as she began communicating with me telepathically, placing her messages directly in my brain, where I would receive them as an inner knowing that was distinct from my own thinking. Being a fast typist, I had no difficulty recording her words as I received them.

Recording my sexual experiences with my partner, however, surprised me. While in the past I'd had little if any recall of my sexual experiences, now my memory of sexual events was excellent and quite detailed. I would generally record our encounters the following day and have my partner review them to be sure I'd represented him accurately and hadn't forgotten anything. Most of the time, he agreed 100 percent with what I'd described. I attributed my new-found clarity of recall to higher forces assisting me.

This book chronicles the entire period of time in 2012 during which I received and implemented Mary's messages about sacred sexuality. To familiarize the reader with my background, the book opens with a brief summary of my spiritual journey and earlier encounters with Mary. It is then divided into three parts, associated with the beginning, intermediate, and advanced sacred sexuality practices Mary delivered. Many of the chapters in each of these parts conclude with a step-by-step guide to the practices described within them. The book ends with a section entitled "Afterword: Continuing the Journey," followed by "Terms and Their Meanings" and a resource listing for readers wishing to delve further into this subject matter.

I'm deeply grateful for the ecstatic sexual experiences my partner and I had as a result of following Mary's guidance. Yet throughout, I was always aware that Mary's teachings are, first and foremost, practices for spiritual development. As she had explained to me previously:

> Sexuality is a doorway that opens you to union with God. . . . You can learn to expand this doorway through techniques such as Tantra.[4] This is valuable as a support for transforming your physical body, your emotional body, your mental body, and your energy body. In awakened sexuality, you are aligning these bodies and unifying them to open to the Divine. . . . It is a wondrous and beautiful sacrament to engage this with another, one of the great gifts of this realm.[5]

May this book contribute to many people's growth and awakening, as it has to my own. If that occurs, then it will have served Mary's mission in sharing this exquisite form of divine communion.

SUBLIME UNION

How I Was Led to Mary

IT WAS A SUNDAY MORNING in July 2010—my first full day in Santa Fe, New Mexico. I wandered outside and was greeted by a deep blue, cloudless sky. The strong sun was already warming the day. All around me were adobe-style homes in earthy pink colors with soft curves at their edges. The sparse, high-desert vegetation was new to me but subtly appealing.

I'd been on the road for the last four months, allowing myself to be guided by Spirit. Much of that time had been spent helping my aging parents, which I was more than glad to do. But throughout my travels Spirit had become mysteriously mute. As the months passed with no direction as to where my new home was to be, my longing for a landing place steadily grew. I wanted to begin the next phase of my life, in which I hoped facilitating people's spiritual growth would become my full-time occupation. In particular, I yearned to be able to channel at will, to become a "voice" of Spirit whenever I wanted so I could offer this service dependably to myself and others. Driving into Santa Fe in the late afternoon the day before, I sensed I'd arrived at a holy city. Light was streaming down from the sky, bathing the buildings and land in golden-white rays of luminosity that were both beautiful and inviting. *Perhaps this is a sign that I've found my destination*, I thought.

Walking back into the casita I was staying in, I wondered what I would do in this unfamiliar city. I wasn't left in the dark for long. Within a few minutes, I received a message from Spirit: "Go to Santa Fe Community Church." How interesting! I'd only been moved to go to a church on extremely rare occasions, usually to accompany someone else, and had consistently found it unfulfilling. This was definitely intriguing.

By the time I located the church, the service was nearly over. I toyed with not going inside so as not to make a disturbance with my entry. But I don't take messages from Spirit lightly, and I assumed there was a reason I'd been directed to come on that morning. I entered quietly and was met at the door by a beautiful white-haired man, whose beaming blue eyes and welcoming smile had the depth and openness of a shining heart. I'd arrived in time for the closing medley of songs, which was perfect as I love to sing. (Later it occurred to me that Spirit had choreographed my late arrival to ensure my entrance would coincide with the part of the service I'd be most attracted to.)

After the singing ended, I was hugged and enthusiastically welcomed by a number of people. Then the man who'd met me at the door invited me to go to lunch with several other newcomers and the minister, who turned out to be down-to-earth and very engaging. She drew each of us into conversation, inviting us to talk about ourselves and informing us of church members who shared our interests. By the end of lunch I had several new friends and a place to live.

Three days later while meditating at my new home, I became aware of an exquisite presence around me. The presence seemed especially strong at my throat, where I sensed I was blocking it from coming through. Wanting it to come forth, I put all my intention on releasing whatever was obstructing its emergence. Suddenly, an unfamiliar voice started speaking through me, and I received an internal communication announcing that it was the voice of Mary Magdalene. She proceeded to deliver an amazing discourse, packed with illuminating instruction on how people could evolve at this pivotal time in our history. By the end of her talk, I had dissolved into a puddle of wonder and bliss.

Little did I know that over the next month Mary would continue to come to me daily with equally enlightening messages. Throughout that time, it was as though I'd been transported to another realm— I was not only receiving Mary's words but also lifted into her ecstatic state of being, where the frequency I usually resonated at was suddenly bumped up several octaves. I felt carried on a wave of rapturous communion yet fully grounded. It was truly a state of grace.

These daily visitations from Mary Magdalene were markedly different from previous messages I'd received from Spirit. The earlier ones had been simple directives, telling me to take a particular action. For instance, months before, toward the end of 2009, I was told telepathically that it was time for me to leave the Big Island of Hawaii, where I'd been living for ten years, thinking it would remain my beloved tropical residence for the rest of my life. As much as I didn't want to go, I knew that whenever I followed instruction from Spirit things inevitably worked out for the best. So I wrapped up my life in Hawaii, finally uprooting myself in March of 2010 to let Spirit guide me to my new home.

What was different about the transmissions I was receiving from Mary Magdalene in Santa Fe was that they weren't just for me. They were universal instructions that applied to many people. And rather than focusing on actions I was to take, they were deeply meaningful spiritual discourses. Soon after Mary initiated her series of visits to me, I realized she was downloading a book, chapter by chapter, which would become *Mary Magdalene Beckons: Join the River of Love*, book one of The Magdalene Teachings.

Although many people think of Mary Magdalene as a Christian figure, I related to her on a very different basis. Having been raised in a Jewish family and having chosen to follow an eclectic, primarily Eastern spiritual path as an adult, I wasn't attached to any particular set of beliefs about her. I simply experienced her as a powerful and wise being representing the Divine Feminine and devoted to serving humanity's spiritual evolution.

However, I came to see that many experiences throughout my life had prepared me perfectly for our work together. They began with visions I'd had at the age of twelve, in which I would see Jesus in the desert of ancient Palestine surrounded by a following of about a hundred people. Although I was not part of his inner circle, I was there walking with Jesus. I remembered his sandals, robe-like clothing, longish hair, and the arid ground beneath us, as well as the powerful attraction everyone in the group felt to his loving, penetrating energy. And I recalled the sense of trust and devotion the group felt toward Jesus as the instrument of a divinely inspired mission.

My visions of Jesus and the gathering around him were always the same and occurred only when I was alone. I never spoke of them, not because I doubted their reality but because I didn't know anyone who would understand, including my Jewish parents. Eventually the visions receded to the back of my consciousness, and for a long time I forgot all about them.

Another set of experiences that prepared me for my engagement with Mary Magdalene involved my longtime embrace of the Feminine aspects of spirituality, including sexuality. After exploring various forms of Eastern spirituality in my teens and early twenties, I became a devotee of an unconventional American guru who openly embraced sexuality as part of the spiritual journey. After seventeen years of active participation in his spiritual community, I was led to another teacher, whose first words to me were, "You're a powerful Tantrica, but you're not utilizing your sexual energy appropriately, so it's backing up in you. This may cause serious problems for you if you don't change the course you're on of holding back your energy." A Tantrica, I knew, was a practitioner of Tantra, a body of ancient Indian spiritual practices that included sexuality as an avenue of oneness with the Divine.

My work with my second teacher focused on reclaiming the parts of myself I was divorced from, especially accepting and integrating my emotional and sexual power. Four months into that teaching I went through a profound awakening: at the core of my being I became all of "who I am"—a being undeniably connected to God in every aspect of myself. And I knew that my awakening had everything to do with having become my full emotional-sexual self.

A third series of events that laid the foundation for my visitations from Mary Magdalene involved connecting with past-life memories and abilities. A Native American shaman told me at age forty-three, "You have a natural ability to cross between the worlds. Many people are working very hard to achieve what comes easily to you." The following year, a psychic saw me in a past life at an ancient Greek temple, where I was an oracle. Later, an astrologer explained that I had the chart of a temple priestess who, in previous incarnations, had been responsible for training other priestesses.

My biggest breakthrough in connecting with my past came in the year 2000. I had just returned to Northern California after living in Hawaii for a year. A woman I knew from Hawaii was leading a communication workshop that I wanted to attend. But, with no job and only limited funds, I couldn't afford the fee. So I approached the workshop host, a local Tantra teacher, who offered me a work exchange for the training. Apparently she liked me because afterward she offered me a job. Two weeks later she invited me to move into her home. And a month after that she threw a party and introduced me to her many friends in the Tantra community.

Soon I was included in all the local Tantra gatherings, especially the insider ones. Then I started getting invitations from teachers to assist or colead at their workshops. They were noticing the same thing I was—that I seemed to be highly skilled at sacred sexuality. But how could that be? My only previous exposure to Tantra had involved the rudimentary techniques I'd learned years before with my first spiritual teacher. Slowly it dawned on me that I'd been a temple priestess long ago, when sacred sexuality was a venerated part of spiritual life and practitioners were supported and honored within the temple system. It also occurred to me that sacred sexuality was the wisdom I had come to share in this lifetime.

Eventually I began leading my own sacred sexuality workshops, first in California and then in Hawaii. The response of participants was overwhelmingly positive, with profuse acclaim for how much my instruction benefited them. Even those experienced in Tantra told me they learned things from me that they hadn't from anyone else.

The final link paving the way for my visits from Mary Magdalene in Santa Fe occurred in 2008, when I read *The Magdalen Manuscript: The Alchemies of Horus & the Sex Magic of Isis* by Tom Kenyon and Judi Sion. In this book, Mary Magdalene revealed that she was a priestess in the Egyptian temple of Isis. She was trained in the sex magic of Isis in preparation for her marriage with Yeshua. They performed these sexual practices together as part of their spiritual work, ultimately empowering Yeshua to fulfill his spiritual mission. While this path had been held in strictest secrecy by initiates, Isis had instructed Mary Magdalene that it was time to make the practices accessible to everyone, saying that those who were meant to have them would know what to do with them.

I read with interest Mary's simple descriptions of Egyptian sacred sexuality, all of which seemed new to me. To my amazement, while reading each practice I experienced a full-blown activation of it within me. By the end of the book, it was clear that I was reliving past-life memories. I, too, had been trained in these practices and my body still remembered them.

As I recalled my roots in the temple of Isis, my long-buried childhood visions of ancient Palestine resurfaced. Suddenly they made complete sense. I realized I had known Mary Magdalene, as well as Mother Mary, because we had all been priestesses of Isis together. I had been drawn to follow Jesus through my earlier ties with his closest family members.

Not long after, Isis herself began coming to me, directing me to offer a priestess-training program for women. I was reluctant to do this because I was still in the process of remembering my own priestess background. Yet Isis assured me she would give me everything I needed. And indeed she did. On the morning of each gathering, she would make her presence felt to me, giving me detailed instructions on what I was to do that evening. The priestess training turned into a yearlong program, with all the women concurring that the instruction was most valuable.

Fortified by this web of preparatory experiences and connections with Mary Magdalene, I welcomed her appearance to me in Santa Fe in July 2010. Nonetheless, I still didn't understand why I'd been brought to this particular location, since Mary could have communicated with me no matter where I was. *Had Spirit relocated me to be close to my family, so I could help my parents? Would the Santa Fe community offer support I would need in becoming one of Mary's representatives? Or was there another reason that wasn't yet obvious?*

Two years later I began to comprehend the design that was under way. Mary had more in store for me and was biding her time for the right moment to begin.

PART I

Beginning Practices

ONE

Mary Beckons Again

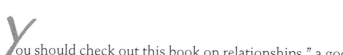

You should check out this book on relationships," a good friend suggested one day in July 2012. "It's written for women, and it might help you."

I definitely needed some help. My lover for the past six months had just dropped a quiet bombshell: he told me that he considered me only a friend. When I heard those words, I went cold inside. The syllables resounded within me like a metal ball bouncing off a steel wall: *I am only his friend.* In that moment, my feelings became crystal clear. "Tony, I want to be more than friends; I want to be partners," I told him earnestly.

He was very understanding and received my feelings openly, responding, "I realize that's what you want. But I can't do that." I knew his answer before he'd said it. He had been clear from day one that he wasn't looking for a relationship. Yet I was still hoping things would be different, that he would have changed. But he hadn't, and I felt devastated.

Maybe the book would help. Plunging in, I found the author's recommendations thought provoking. She said that if you want to be in a committed relationship and your partner doesn't, you should end the relationship and not have any contact. She advised giving the man thirty days to process what had occurred. By the end of thirty days, he would either choose to be with you and commit, or he had already moved on—and so should you.

I figured it was worth a try: I would go cold turkey and have no contact with Tony. It felt like the right thing to do—at least I'd be taking care of myself. And if I poured myself into my work perhaps I wouldn't feel the hole his departure would leave in my life. My first book, *Mary Magdalene Beckons: Join the River of Love,* had been released the previous month, and I had plenty of things to keep me busy in actively promoting it.

One of the more exciting things I embarked on at that time, which helped lift my spirits, was being interviewed on radio shows. I was quite nervous before my first interview. The host was a gregarious woman in Australia who suggested I have a glass of wine before the show to calm my nerves. She obviously didn't know how drunk I get on one glass of wine! I went on the air sober, and fortunately for both of us the interview went very well. After that, radio interviews were a breeze. I discovered I was a natural public speaker. My passion for Mary Magdalene and the teaching she had given me, combined with the unusual experiences that had led me to write the book, made for lots of juicy bits to discuss. The radio hosts seemed to love having me as a guest.

Launching my book wasn't the only thing keeping me busy. Seven months earlier, on New Year's Eve, my eighty-four-year-old father had taken a fall and broken his hip at his home in Albuquerque, New Mexico. The next day he was operated on and then sent to a rehab facility to learn to walk again. At least, that was the plan. But after several weeks of therapy he still wasn't able to walk. The doctors concluded that his early-stage dementia had progressed to the point where his brain wasn't giving the right signals to his legs to get him walking again. Soon we were advised to put him in hospice care as the doctors didn't think he had much longer to live.

My stepmother located an assisted living facility for my dad, and his hospice care began. Over the next month, all the long-distance family members came to visit, realizing this might be the last time. One month went by, then two, then three, but my father did not seem to be declining. In fact, he stabilized to the point where he no longer qualified for hospice. Now he became simply a resident at the assisted living facility, still unable to get out of bed. Amazingly good-natured, he became a favorite there, where all the attendants particularly appreciated his sense of humor and obvious intelligence, in spite of his mental decline.

I adopted a routine of driving down from Santa Fe to visit him twice a week. I would sit next to him and hold his hand, tell him about my life and the progress with the book, give him neck and foot massages, read stories to him, and bring him lattes and chocolate chip cookies to enjoy.

As the months turned into half a year, I got to know the caregivers and many of the other residents at the facility. At first, the acrid smells in the corridors and the "walkers" wandering robotically up and down the hallways were depressing, but little by little I became acquainted with the patients and even fond of them. No longer put off by their behaviors, I started to see their humanity shining through. I appreciated how they were stretching my heart open in new ways, making room for the sick and disadvantaged and forgotten.

When my father's birthday came around that summer, we organized a celebration for him. As a special present, his favorite caregiver had arranged to have four able-bodied attendants transfer him into a wheelchair and, for the first time since his arrival six months earlier, he was able to leave his room. We wheeled him outdoors to take in the air and sunshine, then into the community room for a songfest and sharing of birthday cake, where he had a great time with the other residents.

A week later my dad couldn't remember any of it. He was back in bed and none of us knew what the future held—least of all my father, whose concept of past and future were quickly disappearing. We were all learning to receive one of the gifts of dementia—the ability to live in the present.

All these things kept me busy once I had decided to let go of my relationship with Tony. But I never forgot him, and I carefully tracked the passage of time without him. Almost like clockwork, he called me on day thirty. "Mercedes, I'm missing you terribly," he confessed. "I'd really like to see you. Would you like to go out to dinner together?" That night while sitting next to each other at our favorite restaurant, we ordered our usual enchilada dishes and talked about how hard it was to be apart. By the end of the meal we were back together.

At last my world seemed whole again. I continued promoting my book and visiting my father, but now Tony was texting, calling, and visiting regularly or taking me out. Even though our physical attraction was as strong as ever, I decided to hold off on being sexual until I was sure we were creating the kind of partnership I wanted. Tony understood and seemed happy to just be spending time together, as was I.

One of the radio-show hosts who interviewed me at that time was a woman who also channeled Mary Magdalene. We felt a strong connection with each other, and after the interview she suggested we do a trade, each of us channeling Mary for the other. I liked the idea, and we scheduled my session for receiving a channeled message for mid-August. I had received a channeling from someone only once before and, while curious about what would come through, certainly wasn't prepared for what I would be told or for the events it would set in motion.

The channeling began with Mary thanking me for the work I'd

done on my first book. She said much had been written about her that was untrue but I had brought the beautiful energy of her words into print. She also expressed concern that I was pushing myself too hard and needed to relax. She said she wanted me to begin a forty-four day retreat during which I was to rest. But that wasn't all. During the forty-four days, she said, we would begin the next phase of our work together: she would start instructing me in sacred sexuality in preparation for a new book she was ready to deliver. She assured me that she would give me everything I needed.

Then she invited me to take her hand and walk with her on the Sea of Galilee, calling that body of water transformative and magical. She guided me to feel the wind blow across my face and into my hair and to allow my heart to open, my mind to be healed, and my body to come to rest. She said that in future meetings we would continue to walk together upon the water, and she would begin to whisper her wisdom in my heart.

Mary's final words during that channeling were both profound and deeply sobering:

You will receive information about the sacred connection between heaven and earth, and the kundalini in male-female.[1] You will bring sacred sensuality back onto this planet. You are changing how the world will respond not only to sexuality in terms of male-female but to the energy of passion and cocreation that is deep within each one, so that individuals may no longer be victims but instead empowered within themselves.

This is the story I wish to share with you and to bear with you, since you will be birthing a new energy as we speak. This is about the energy of the Divine within you. It is about cocreating with God.[2] The story that you will bring forth will empower individuals' passionate connection to God through sacred sexuality. This is everyone's birthright as a child of God.

I was deeply moved by Mary's invitation to walk with her on the Sea of Galilee, to receive her personal instruction in sacred sexuality, and to bring forth a story that would birth a new energy in the world! My mind was reeling, yet my heart was calm and clear. I was being asked to make yet another leap of faith—to let go of shepherding my first book all the way through its emergence into the world, trusting that higher forces were at work supporting its success.

In truth, I couldn't imagine turning Mary down and all she was offering. My heart knew as soon as I heard her words what I would do. By the end of the channeling, my course was altered. Heartened by the promise of magic and transformation, I was ready to heed Mary's call. And I was especially excited about sharing the journey with Tony.

TWO

Divine Appointment

had met Tony two years earlier, in July 2010, shortly after my arrival in Santa Fe. Following my first week of interacting almost exclusively with Mary Magdalene, I was hungry for an infusion of human contact. I returned to Santa Fe Community Church, whose fellowship had received me so graciously the previous Sunday. I resonated with parts of the sermon and, once again, heartily enjoyed the singing. What I most appreciated, though, was the feeling of community among the members. As everyone exchanged hugs at the end of the service, I felt genuinely embraced and welcomed. One woman told me how beautiful my singing was and invited me to join the choir. Though I'd never been in a choir before, it sounded like fun.

The service was followed by a picnic, so I wandered outside. There at the grill was a striking-looking man—very Hispanic, with huge bushy eyebrows and warm brown eyes. He said hello and smiled. I introduced myself. He said his name was Antonio but everyone called him Tony. We spoke briefly and all the while he gazed at me with a gently penetrating look.

After the picnic, I stepped into the sanctuary to attend the choir rehearsal I'd been invited to. Scanning the members of the choir, I recognized only two of them—the woman who'd invited me and

Tony—both of whom greeted me amiably and told me where to sit. I have a high singing range, and everyone seemed delighted to have a new soprano in the choir because they'd had a shortage of people singing in that register. I fully enjoyed paticipating with the group and looked forward to the next service in which we'd be singing.

Being in the choir kept me returning to the church. While I didn't wholly agree with the philosophy, it was close enough to my own that I could receive its offerings openheartedly. I enjoyed the friends I was making there, and seeing the faces of the congregation light up in response to our singing was exhilarating.

That fall, Tony and I became better acquainted. The church had organized study groups to read and discuss a book about blessing others. The group that matched my schedule was one that Tony had already joined. Meeting with the group week after week, I became moved by his kindness and the depth to which he opened himself to the blessing practice. He would describe waking up early in the morning—often around 3:00 or 4:00—calling to mind all the people he knew and blessing them, sometimes for hours at a time. His caring and sincerity impressed me.

My own spiritual growth was also blossoming during that time. I'd discovered that I was able to communicate not only with Mary Magdalene but with many higher beings. Consequently, I started to offer private sessions in which I channeled clients' personal guides or angels. These sessions proved to be powerful, but I wanted to do more. I began to schedule monthly gatherings for channeling whatever higher being was moved to communicate through me for the highest good of all. The messages that came through were profound and timely commentaries from Mary Magdalene, Yeshua, Mother Mary, Isis, Archangel Michael, and, over time, many others.

As my work gradually unfolded, Tony kept showing up—first

asking for a reading, then coming to events I was leading. At one point, he asked, "Would you like to go out to lunch and get to know each other better?" And so our friendship began.

We found we had a great deal in common. Tony was slow to open up about himself, but I came to realize that his spiritual path was at least as deep and powerful as mine. I enjoyed having someone who understood me to the core of my being, especially from a spiritual perspective. We could talk about anything together, and our values and ideas were complementary. But what really stood out was how much fun we had. We would laugh and laugh together. Everything felt easy and light in each other's company. And we noticed that food always tasted more delicious than usual during the meals we shared.

Of course, that wasn't all we noticed. There was no denying that we were attracted to each other. It was palpable, like electricity. We talked about that, too. And here we finally found our difference. I wanted to be in a relationship, but Tony was not looking for that. So we kept our attraction confined to juicy hugs and more-than-friendly kisses.

Months passed as I made progress on writing my first book. By August 2011, the manuscript was complete and I entered into the production phase of self-publishing, overseeing countless tasks, juggling dozens of time lines, and learning daily by the seat of my pants. I was fully committed to providing whatever I could of my time, talent, and resources to serve Mary's work in the world, trusting that I would be taken care of in the process.

My hope was to have the book out in time for Christmas sales. I believed that people needed to receive Mary's instructions then so they'd have a year to prepare for the fast-approaching turning point of December 21, 2012, the date proposed by an ever-growing chorus of New Age voices as the end date of the Mayan calendar. Many spiritual traditions and prophecies seemed to corroborate the importance of that date as being a time of either great destruction or profound transformation or both, depending on their point of view. Although I didn't know what was going to happen on December 21 of the following year, I did sense that something of great consequence was under way, and I certainly didn't want to be the cause of people not having all the information they required to go through that gateway.

My response was to dig in and work as fast and furiously as I could. By October 2011, it was obvious that my Christmas-season release date was a pipe dream. By November, I was feeling overwhelmed. In early December, I started sliding into a depression. There was simply more to do than I could handle, and something inside me was going numb. One of my friends gave me flower essence remedies, which would buoy me but only for a few days. While everyone I knew seemed to be busy with holiday festivities, I fell deeper and deeper into my hole. Finally, another friend came to visit and became worried about the state he found me in. He sat me down, looked me in the eyes, and said, "What do you need that would help you?"

My mind felt fuzzy and I could hardly focus. But my friend persisted. Slowly I started to connect my brain to my feelings, and I replied, "Being touched." Then I expanded that to "I would like to have a partner to be in relationship with." From there I got really specific: "I need some sex!"

My friend didn't flinch or relax his gaze. "Well, do you know anyone you could have sex with?" Now here was a novel idea! Immediately, three people came to mind. With a bit more thought, I ruled out two of them, which left Tony.

Tony would understand, I told myself. *We've talked about sex, just like we've talked about everything, and we're in amazing agreement. Even*

though he doesn't want to be in a relationship, we could be friends with ben-
efits. Good friends—and maybe the benefits will be just as good. It certainly
is worth a try.

I can't remember how I opened the door to becoming intimate. I must have told Tony I was depressed and needed help. I probably invited him to sleep over. All I know is that in no time we went from buddies to lovers. And it was wonderful.

Now the world had a bit of a glow. My challenges didn't feel so overwhelming because Tony was with me. He believed in me even when I didn't. He told me again and again how important my work was and what a good job I was doing. And he gently reminded me to take breaks and have fun.

We were extremely good at having fun. Eating together was fun. Cooking together was fun. Going out to restaurants together was fun. Laughing together was fun. Spending time with his kids and grandkids, going dancing, hiking in the mountains—it was all fun. And our lovemaking was more than fun. It was nourishment and passion and deep connection. We would make love for hours, taking a break and starting up again, until we were deeply satisfied. Then Tony would go home.

I remember lying in bed, happily watching him get dressed. Like many Hispanic men, Tony's taste in clothing was superb, and he always made a point of dressing well. His body was hot, from his large barrel chest to his amazingly slim hips, and he always looked gorgeous to me. I watched him slither into his tight black jeans, button up his beautifully fitted shirt, slide into his expensive boots, and put on his rings, bracelet, watch, and necklace. He would finish with combing his shoulder-length hair, tying it back, and smoothing his beard and mustache. Then he'd lean over and give me a long kiss and hug, which I would totally drink in. I'd wrap my robe around myself and walk him to the door, feeling like the most beautiful courtesan in the world. We'd share one last lingering embrace and kiss, then I'd send him off into the night and return to my bed to a deliciously deep sleep.

Months flew by. By June 2012, *Mary Magdalene Beckons* was ready to be released, just in time for me to do a book signing at the International New Age Trade Show in Denver. I asked Tony if he'd like to join me, and he said he would.

We passed the time on the drive to Denver listening to my playlist of classic rock and roll from the sixties, seventies, and eighties. Tony knew all the artists and most of the lyrics, and we had fun singing together and reminiscing over the memories the music evoked.

I'd never been to a new age trade show before, so this was an initiation into a whole new world for me. I found that people were very interested in Mary Magdalene and my book. When it was time for my book signing, so many people lined up that I went a half hour over my time slot autographing books. I also networked with the other vendors, made many valuable connections, and signed on with a distributor to sell my book to bookstores and new age shops.

Tony was having a good time exploring all the different items on display and connecting with different people. I was glad he was enjoying himself, but I also felt a bit disappointed. I'd envisioned Tony spending time with me and the two of us doing things together at the show. Although he was very supportive of me during my book signing, the rest of the time he was content being on his own, exploring the show, which left me on my own as well. When our paths would occasionally cross and we'd be together for a while, it felt more like a coincidence than a choice.

Something else was bothering me, too. When I introduced Tony to other people, I didn't know what to call him. I considered him my lover, but that felt too intimate and unprofessional to say to people. Nor did I feel comfortable calling him my boyfriend because that seemed kind of high-schoolish. "Significant other" sounded cumbersome and somewhat weird. The only other term I could think of was "partner," but I didn't feel like he was my partner.

On the morning we were leaving to drive back, I told Tony my dilemma. "I feel confused about how to introduce you to others," I shared. "What do you call me when you're talking about me to other people?"

His reply was simple: "I say you're my friend."

A tidal wave of sadness washed over me, leaving me empty and dazed. Tony had confirmed what I already instinctively knew but hadn't wanted to admit. Over the months, my heart had opened to him, and now I was in love. I wanted more than friendship. But unfortunately, he didn't.

I needed to be alone, to take care of myself, to protect my hurting heart. I went into the hotel-room bathroom, closed the door, undressed, and started a hot shower. As the water poured over my head and shoulders, I let out the tears I'd been holding back. I cried and cried until there were none left. And then I became calm.

Emerging from the bathroom, I noticed the room was empty. Tony had collected the luggage and was loading the truck. When he returned, we gathered the rest of our things, checked out of the hotel, and headed back to Santa Fe.

Tony drove as I silently cried for the first hour, grateful that we both were comfortable enough to not feel a need to fix me. By the time we got to Colorado Springs, I was done with my emotional outpouring. Feeling grateful for the solidity of our friendship, I began to engage Tony in light conversation. We eventually stopped for lunch at a place where I had the most delicious pizza of my life. Emotional release certainly cleanses the taste buds!

As we pulled into my driveway that evening, I felt peaceful. We unloaded my gear from the truck and said good-bye. Then it hit me:

I was alone. After spending the last five days with Tony, I was now all by myself. I had a sinking feeling in the pit of my stomach as I vacantly set about putting my things away. By the time I'd finished, I was tired. I cocooned into the familiar comfort of my bed, welcoming sleep as an escape from the emptiness I felt inside.

It was one week later, after reading the book recommended by my friend, that I ended my relationship with Tony, and thirty days after that we recommenced.

Now, in mid-August, Mary had just announced I was to go on a forty-four day retreat and begin a new book with her. I had no idea what was in store.

THREE

Receiving the Light

My forty-four-day retreat with Mary started immediately, which didn't surprise me, as I knew she was ready to go. In the higher realms, everything seems to happen in the "now."

She began her communication speaking very personally and specifically to me.

Blessings, dear one,

You are very sensitive, and you are not taking care of yourself in the way you need to. You must live in a temple. Do you realize this? You require a temple environment. Everyone does, but you are extremely sensitive to your surroundings. So you must clean your space and maintain it in that condition. You must bring everything into order, especially around your office and your financial matters—even your will. And you must make your environment beautiful, as a temple is beautiful. This is not hard for you. You must serve your environment and bring in the sacred. This is also not hard for you. So that is the first order of business for you to handle.

You must connect with nature every day for at least a half hour. You must make this a priority. In the past, growing a garden supported you in connecting with the Earth. Now you must find another way.

Finally, you must tend to your body through exercise every day. This is not optional; it is required.

These are the things you must bring into alignment in your life. This will give you the base, the platform, the necessary foundation for you to move forward.

I was grateful for Mary's clear instruction. I knew she was referring to a basic understanding in the temples we'd both served in long ago. Since I no longer lived in that kind of formal setting, I needed to actively set the stage for inviting in the Divine, with its accompanying otherworldly and transformative powers. These were indeed areas I needed to address to make my home and my body empowered and sacred containers for the Divine. My messy desk, financial disarray, procrastination in creating a will, lack of exercise, and dissociation from the Earth were all "black holes" where energy was leaking out of my vessel. Attending to them would make my home and body strong and clear portals for receiving Mary's messages.

Having covered these foundational points, Mary continued with her initial instruction to me regarding sacred sexuality.

Come take my hand, dear sister. I will bring you with me, and we will walk on the Sea of Galilee together. Let the wind blow through your hair. Your mind is open. Your body is soft. Roll with the waves. You know how to do this.

The sun shines brightly and connects with your heart. Let your heart receive the light. Light is your heart's sustenance. You cannot love without the light. The light is God's love and the source of your love. Let your heart soften and receive the light.

Let the light spread out to your whole self. Receive the light with your whole self. Do you feel this? I can tell you do. This is the essence of Tantra—receiving light with your whole self. Sexual energy is simply a particular frequency of light in the body. It is good to receive light in your heart first and then let it spread to your whole self. This is the woman's way.

Mercedes: Is it the same for men?

It is slightly different for men. The Masculine way is to receive energy first through the genitals, and from there the energy awakens the heart. For the Masculine, it is not so easy, initially, to feel the heart. I am speaking about the Masculine rather than "men" because some men are very connected to their Feminine. This doesn't mean they are unmanly; it simply means they are more balanced.

The Masculine most often accesses the heart through the genitals. So, compared with the Feminine, it is often not as immediate for the Masculine to connect with the heart. This is one reason why the Masculine is drawn to the Feminine. Through the Feminine (most often in the form of women), the Masculine can connect with the heart. It is a natural attraction. As the Masculine comes into balance with the Feminine within, the individual increasingly has the capacity to find that balance within. Then that being has natural access to all the parts of themselves, including the heart, the brain, and the body. This is what you are all growing toward. You will be more harmonious with yourself and others the more you achieve this.

To arrive at this internal wholeness, it is very important that the heart and sacral chakras be connected.[1] In response to sexual energy, the Feminine tends to have the heart chakra open and the sacral chakra closed, whereas the Masculine tends to have the sacral chakra open and the heart chakra closed. Both have work to do to have both the sacral and heart chakras open and connected.

There's also balancing work to be done within the sacral chakra itself. The Feminine tends to have the sacral chakra open to emotional energy, while the Masculine tends to have the sacral chakra open to sexual energy. The optimum is to have the sacral chakra open to both emotional and sexual energy.

Mercedes: Is a corresponding balance needed within the heart chakra? Is there a way the Masculine is open at the heart and the Feminine is closed?

The balancing you're referring to occurs between the brain and the heart. The Masculine is more open in the brain, and the Feminine is more open in the heart.

Mercedes: What about intuition and psychic abilities at the third eye chakra?

In general, the Feminine is more naturally open in that way.

Mercedes: Is there a counterpart for the Masculine?

The counterpart for the Masculine occurs in terms of connecting with and resting in consciousness, which is another function of the third eye chakra.

Mercedes: What about the other chakras?

The solar plexus chakra tends to be more open for the Masculine. The counterpart for the Feminine is the connection with the physical body at the root chakra.

Figure 3-1. CHAKRAS—ENERGY CENTERS

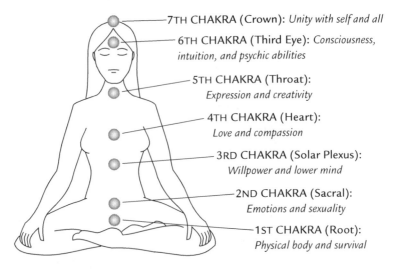

7TH CHAKRA (Crown): *Unity with self and all*

6TH CHAKRA (Third Eye): *Consciousness, intuition, and psychic abilities*

5TH CHAKRA (Throat): *Expression and creativity*

4TH CHAKRA (Heart): *Love and compassion*

3RD CHAKRA (Solar Plexus): *Willpower and lower mind*

2ND CHAKRA (Sacral): *Emotions and sexuality*

1ST CHAKRA (Root): *Physical body and survival*

Mercedes: So it seems the Feminine is naturally more connected to and open in the root chakra, the sacral chakra in terms of emotional energy, the heart chakra, and the third eye chakra in terms of intuition and psychic abilities. The Masculine is more naturally attuned to and open in the sacral chakra in terms of sexuality, the solar plexus chakra in terms of willpower and lower mind, and the third eye chakra in terms of consciousness.

Yes, that is correct. Now rest your mind and feel.

Feel your heart. This is the first step of soothing and coming to peace and rest.

Now feel your sacral chakra, and feel it connected to your heart.

When that is strong and full, add your root chakra. Rest in this.

That is enough for now.

Rest in this, dear one, and let it continue throughout your day. When you lose the connection and openness, gently bring yourself back to it, through awareness, feeling, and intention.

I leave you with this for the first lesson of practice.

I love you. I kiss your hair, gladden your heart, and touch your feet.

In love, your dear sister,
Mary Magdalene

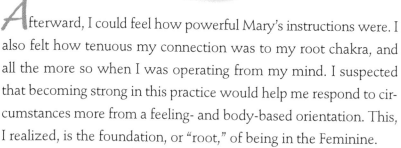

Afterward, I could feel how powerful Mary's instructions were. I also felt how tenuous my connection was to my root chakra, and all the more so when I was operating from my mind. I suspected that becoming strong in this practice would help me respond to circumstances more from a feeling- and body-based orientation. This, I realized, is the foundation, or "root," of being in the Feminine.

I engaged this practice intentionally the rest of the day and even after going to bed, when it became yet more powerful as I was less distracted. I had so much energy as a result of following Mary's instruction that I didn't fall asleep until 5:00 a.m.!

At one point during the night, I began wondering if Mary recommended the same practice for men. I decided to ask her in one of our upcoming sessions.

Later that night I remembered the Taoist "Inner Smile" technique, an exercise I had learned many years ago in which the practitioner connects with their internal energy starting at the sacral chakra, moves to the heart chakra, then returns to the sacral chakra. As I lay awake during the early morning hours, I started experimenting with my own synthesis of the Taoist technique and Mary's instruction, telling myself:

> Visualize a smile radiating out in all directions from your heart. Let this heart-radiating smile become strong and deep. Continue radiating the smile as you shift your focus to your sacral chakra. Visualize a flower, possibly a rose with no thorns, at your sacral chakra. Because this chakra is associated with orange, visualize the rose as orange, peach, coral, or yellow with reddish tips, then see it opening in all directions. Feel the softness of its petals at your sacral chakra, and smell its delicate scent. Let this experience become strong and deep. Continue connecting with your heart and sacral chakra as you shift your focus to your root chakra. Visualize a rainbow at your root chakra, shining rays of colored light out in all directions.

I found this form of the practice to be potent and subtly pleasurable. The more I practiced it, the more my ability to open my lower chakras expanded.

To my surprise, the next day I had much more energy than I would have expected after a night of so little sleep. I felt alive and excited to see what was next, and eager to share the first practice with Tony.

Figure 3-2. AWAKENING THE HEART, SACRAL, AND ROOT CHAKRAS

1. Let your heart soften and receive the light of God's love. Let the light spread throughout your entire being. Receive the light with your whole self.

2. Feel your heart. Let this bring you to peace and rest.

3. Feel your sacral chakra. Feel it connected to your heart chakra. Let the connection between your sacral chakra and heart chakra become full and strong.

4. While continuing with step 3, feel your root chakra. Feel it connected to your heart chakra. Let the connection between your root chakra and heart chakra become full and strong.

5. Feel your root and sacral chakras simultaneously, with both connected to your heart chakra. Rest in this feeling.

6. Let this feeling continue throughout your day. Whenever you lose the connection and openness between your heart, sacral, and root chakras, gently bring yourself back to it through awareness, feeling, and intention.

Figure 3-3. VARIATION ON AWAKENING THE HEART, SACRAL, AND ROOT CHAKRAS

Contributed by Mercedes Kirkel

1. Visualize a smile radiating out in all directions from your heart. Let this visualization become strong and deep.

2. Continue radiating the smile from your heart as you shift your focus to your sacral chakra. Visualize a flower, possibly a rose with no thorns, at your sacral chakra. Because this chakra is associated with orange, visualize the rose as orange, peach, coral, or yellow with reddish tips, then see it opening in all directions. Feel the softness of its petals at your sacral chakra, and smell its delicate scent. Let this experience become strong and deep.

3. Continue connecting with your heart and sacral chakra as you shift your focus to your root chakra. Visualize a rainbow at your root chakra, shining rays of colored light out in all directions.

FOUR

Waters of the Womb

On the second day of my forty-four-day retreat, my stepmother, Margaret, was preparing for back surgery. She'd been making arrangements for the period covering her operation, which was to take place in four days, and subsequent rehab, ensuring that all my dad's needs would be tended to in her absence. When I received a call from her that evening, I figured she wanted to talk about some practical detail she needed help with. But the tone in her voice told me otherwise. "Mercedes, your dad was having seizures and we think he had a stroke," she told me. "He's at the university hospital emergency room. I'm headed over there right now."

I dropped everything, grabbed a few essentials, not knowing how long I'd be in Albuquerque, and jumped in my car to join her at the hospital. The drive flew by, and before I knew it I was entering the emergency room. My dad was conscious but not able to talk. I kissed him, held his hand, and began praying for whatever was for his highest good.

The doctor came in and determined that my dad appeared to have an infection. Tests were ordered, which we knew from previous visits would probably take most of the night to complete. Then the doctor spoke with us privately out in the hall. "It's likely he won't make it through the night," he warned us as gently as possible.

My stepmother looked the doctor in the eye and, flashing back on my dad's previous medical emergencies, said, "We've heard that before. You may be right, but I wouldn't count on it. He's stronger than any of us would have guessed." In that moment, I was impressed with her strength.

After a few hours of sitting with my father, Margaret and I retired to her house for some sleep, instructing the staff to call if anything changed. Returning to the hospital in the morning, we were met with more hopeful news. The tests showed that my dad's infection was the cause of his seizures. If he did have a stroke, it had been mild, with no apparent side effects.

My dad spent most of the next few days sleeping. Upon waking, he would be confused, unable to talk easily, often speaking in loops, repeating the same phrase over and over. He seemed to be conversing with beings we weren't aware of, immersed in his own world of memories or perhaps dreams.

As it turned out, my next two weeks would be largely devoted to caring for him and for Margaret during her recovery from the surgery. I couldn't help but think that Mary knew all this was about to happen—perhaps it was why she told me to relax and go on retreat.

Throughout those two weeks, Mary communicated with me four times. Her first transmission was again very personal:

Dear one,

Blessings and love from your spiritual guide and sister, Mary Magdalene.

I come again to you. It has been several days, as you have been serving your family in the latest health crisis with your father. Your service and love are good and strong—they are two of your strengths. Yet I tell you there is more you can do. You can remain more connected to God in the midst of these times. You do this through your attention—through prayer, repeating your mantra, or whatever else keeps your attention with God.[1] You can also do this energetically, through your breath and feeling—especially feeling your heart, along with your sacral and root chakras.

You tend to practice strongly when you are in pain or very difficult circumstances. You also are strong when you consciously choose to practice at designated times, such as while meditating. And you naturally practice when you are in a circumstance that supports you, such as being in a sacred place or engaging in sacred activity. But in the other times you tend to go unconscious. That is what you need to change. Do not become serious or heavy about it. Simply hold it as an intention and awareness, and let this behavior transform.

Regarding the Tantric practices I have given you, continue opening to your sacral and root chakras, letting them connect to your heart. You are doing well with this. And there is deeper to go with it.

Now I take you again to the Sea of Galilee. Feel the waves gently lifting and lowering you. Feel their ebb and flow, like that of life itself. Feel the waves lifting and lowering you in your sacral chakra. You knew this feeling in the womb—a time of ecstasy and safety, of immersion in love and light. Remember this feeling in your body and let yourself welcome it. You can come from this feeling when you open to God with another. Your memory of floating in the waters of the womb can be tapped into to enhance your vulnerability and openness in Tantra.

Following a long silence, she continued.

Yes, you are dropping into the depth of this beautiful fourth-dimensional and third-dimensional prebirth space.[2] The developing baby in the womb experiences both dimensions, having come from the between-life space of the fourth dimension and arrived in the physical *realm of the third dimension. Going into the fourth-dimensional Tantric space helps you welcome a child into the world by meeting them in their dimension, which is most supportive for them.*

This is enough for now, dear one.

Blessings and love to you,
Mary Magdalene

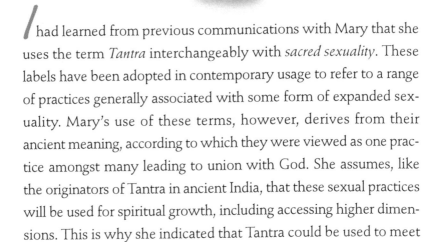

I had learned from previous communications with Mary that she uses the term *Tantra* interchangeably with *sacred sexuality*. These labels have been adopted in contemporary usage to refer to a range of practices generally associated with some form of expanded sexuality. Mary's use of these terms, however, derives from their ancient meaning, according to which they were viewed as one practice amongst many leading to union with God. She assumes, like the originators of Tantra in ancient India, that these sexual practices will be used for spiritual growth, including accessing higher dimensions. This is why she indicated that Tantra could be used to meet a child in their dimension at the time of conception.

I practiced Mary's latest instruction of drawing upon the feeling of being in the womb as I kept my dad company in the hospital. Deep inside, I could feel the connection between my father hovering on the edge of death and Mary's work with me. Both were opening a window for me into the next dimension—a place we experience both before and after our life, as well as through sacred sexuality.

I imagined that just as a fetus continues to experience the fourth dimension while developing in the third dimension, a dying person might also exist in both dimensions. I pictured the fourth dimension as the realm we inhabit between lifetimes, as well as a place we visit in dreams. After we die, we go fully into the fourth dimension to review our life, integrate the lessons we've learned, and make our soul plans and agreements for our next incarnation. I guessed that during his time in the hospital, my father was going more deeply into the fourth dimension than usual.

During my many trips back and forth between Santa Fe and Albuquerque to tend to the myriad of details involving my father and stepmother's health care, I used my driving time to practice the initial exercise Mary had given me. I soon found my engagement of this exercise becoming strong. Staying in my heart, sacral, and root chakras helped me remain in the present and not get lost in my head or "go unconscious," as Mary had put it. Of course, Mary's continuing presence and contact at this time was also a tremendous support.

FIVE

Glimpsing the Higher Dimensions

*T*wo days later, I received the next communication from Mary.

Greetings again, beloved sister,

You are doing well in your progress with the heart chakra, sacral chakra, and root chakra exercise. You can feel how this transforms you in your relationship to life.

You have wondered if this is the same practice given to men, and it is. For men, it primarily encourages an opening at the heart. For both men and women, this exercise opens you to the higher light frequencies through the chakras; these frequencies are generally not experienced without this kind of intentional practice. This is truly the foundation for practicing Tantra.

The early Taoists understood this. The people of old India did too, as did the ancient Egyptians. It remains available to anyone regardless of their culture or religion. This understanding is the basis for moving into fourth-dimensional consciousness. In the fourth dimension, you are relating energetically to all your chakras. All the chakras are necessary for opening the flow of sexual energy, although we have been focusing primarily on the three that hold the most blocks for most people, especially Westerners. Now that most of your world is "Westernized," this is true for most people at this time.

The next step is to focus on the sacral chakra, to breathe into it and begin to feel its specific energies. You may feel the movement or flow of something alive at this energy center, like a serpent that is spiraling or rising. You may see colors, patterns, or visions. You may have images come up, like a movie. Even smells may arise, like the beautiful scent of a rose. Allow it all, and let yourself simply feel it. This exercise can be done as a meditation. Like journeying in the shamanic tradition, let yourself be shown what is there. Have the experience fully. Afterward, it may be valuable to write down your experience or to share it verbally with another.

This is your next practice.

I love you and bless you.
I AM Mary Magdalene

I engaged this instruction throughout the day. As I did, the practice became increasingly easier and more natural.

That evening when I went into my dad's hospital room, he suddenly seemed to have "come back" and was present again. When he saw me, his face lit up with delight and surprise. Then he said with amazement, "I can't believe you're here. I never expected to see you . . ."—a comment he repeated several times.

I'm not sure who he thought I was or where he thought I'd been. I'd visited him every day that week and regularly over the previous two years. Grateful for the opportunity to converse with him, I simply accepted his statements, without needing to know their meaning. In that moment, his "return" was enough.

It was as if he was in a beatific state, radiating happiness and serenity. Even without understanding what he was thinking, I felt graced and blessed to be invited into his reality and become a part of it.

I asked him if he remembered that Margaret had had her surgery that day. He seemed to dimly remember and said, "This was her second."

I replied, "No, it's not her second surgery." Then I thought he might be remembering her surgery from the year before, when she had broken her wrist. Once again, I let go of trying to understand and simply allowed him his perceptions and thoughts.

Mostly we were simply together—my dad in his hospital bed and me on a chair by his side. The joy and love between us was palpable. There wasn't a need for more.

At one point he told me he wasn't remembering much. Feeling his frustration, I reassured him, saying, "It's not what you remember or think that matters. What matters is your heart and the love you feel." He appeared to accept that on a deep level.

Then he looked over my shoulder and seemed to fixate on something very profound. I wondered if he was having a vision. In fact, he was, but not the kind I was imagining. I turned to see what he was looking at and realized it was the white board on the wall, inscribed with his medical information. Slowly he said, "Do you see that board? To me, it's a love board."

I was so moved that I walked over to the board and wrote, "I love you," then signed my name. He seemed extremely pleased, beaming back at me with a wide grin. Then he laughed because directly beneath my message was a reminder to the nurses that he couldn't feed himself. So the whole communication read: "I love you. Mercedes. Please feed me." His joy was so infectious that I began to laugh.

Before I left, we expressed our love to each other. Then I kissed him good-bye, filled to the brim with pure love.

The following morning after checking in on Margaret, who seemed to be doing very well, I drove to the hospital my dad was in and found him more alert than before yet still in an exalted state. He was tracking everything going on around him with wonder and awe. As I stood beside his bed, he asked me to turn around, though I couldn't figure out why. When I turned around, he pointed out the window and said, "Isn't that beautiful?"

I looked out onto an ordinary downtown cityscape of buildings, streets, traffic, and a small patch of grass with a couple of trees. To me it seemed gray and pedestrian. But my father said, with great appreciation, "Isn't that building beautiful? And look at those clouds!"

Normally too busy to notice such things, I allowed my gaze to follow his pointing finger to the building across the street—and I saw it. It was as though my dad had lent me his vision and his capacity to have the experience of awe that he was enjoying.

I felt like I was in the company of an angel. With heightened sensitivity, I saw that there was beauty in the building, which some architect had worked to produce. And there was no question that the clouds were a manifestation of natural splendor. Suddenly everything felt like a miracle. I marveled at the fact that we were surrounded by amazing structures of human invention and creations of nature. I saw magnificence in things I normally didn't notice that made up a world I'd viewed as purely utilitarian. *How easily I take everything for granted*, I told myself. *I'm not even aware of most of existence!*

Later the nurse came in to attend to my father. She emptied his catheter into the toilet and then flushed the contents down. He immediately wanted to know what that sound was. We told him it was the toilet flushing and he responded, with astonishment, "Imagine that!" The nurse and I caught each other's eye and shared a smile, each of us uplifted by his innocent marveling at this otherwise mundane experience.

My dad was aware of every person in and around his room,

wanting to know their name, function, and what they were doing. He remembered that Margaret had had surgery and wanted to know how she was doing. We called her on the phone, and he happily spoke with her. He pointed to the message of love I had written on the white board the day before and seemed very pleased to have that in front of him, reading it aloud again and again.

I tried to find a nurse who could give me more information about his condition. He pointed to a workman who was doing a repair in the hallway and said, "I bet he could help you." At first I thought, *Surely the workman won't be able to help me find the nurse.* But almost immediately I sensed where my father was coming from. He was feeling a profound connection to everything and everyone around him, as though they were all personal gifts from God, who was perfectly providing for him.

At one point I asked him if he was tired, and he said with a feeling of happiness, "As a matter of fact, I am." I told him with a smile, "Let yourself sleep. I'll be right here, working on my computer." He allowed himself to float off to sleep with a childlike innocence that was unusual for this very social person who took great pleasure in interacting with others. I was there for a few more hours, during which he slept and woke with ease several times. It was very sweet and intimate.

As I was leaving the hospital, I reflected on the previous eight months of my father's bedridden state and my impatience with it. I'd often wondered why he was choosing to stay in this realm when there was so little he could do. Why didn't he just let go and transition out of this world into his next phase of life? After this visit, however, I had the thought that maybe he was moving into the higher dimensions in this world rather than transforming through dying. I felt at peace and deeply grateful for what I'd been given. I sensed I'd been with an angel.

Throughout the day, I'd been engaging the practice Mary had given me that morning, all the while connecting with the beauty and femininity of my sacral chakra. As the connection became stronger, I spontaneously began using my eyes to radiate these qualities out to all the people I encountered at the hospital. It felt natural and deeply enjoyable to send out Feminine love and vulnerability by showing who I was and gifting others with the beauty of my essence.

Reflecting further on Mary's message, I wondered whether we shut down in the sacral chakra from wounding or if openness in this energy center is not there at birth and needs to be developed. My guess was that both are true. I thought about how sexual drive could also cover over the sacral chakra's deeper, softer, more vulnerable qualities. Excitement about this new exploration bubbled up inside me, and I felt eager to learn more.

SIX

Activation

*I*t was two days later at 2:30 a.m. I felt filled with sexual energy and couldn't sleep. I tossed and turned in my bed, my mind awake and churning. I thought to myself: *I need a partner to share this energy with. Should I ask Tony to be with me Tantrically? Is that what Mary would want me to do? Is there some other loving partner for me? Should I look for a life partner or a spouse or a Tantric partner?*

Thoughts and questions endlessly coursed through my mind, interwoven with sexual energy that was alive and activated, keeping me up. *What should I do? Should I engage in practice? Should I recite my mantra? Should I do Tantric practice?*

Then the answer came: "Relax." It felt like it was from Mary.

I instantly understood—I needed to let go of all my *doing* and simply *be*.

I followed the instruction and completely relaxed. Suddenly my body opened in powerful orgasms. Charged waves of energy surged through me from my root chakra to my crown, undulating my whole body in strong spasms. Afterward I felt the energetic column that runs from the root chakra through the crown, also referred to as the "central channel," buzzing with an activated vibration, connecting all my chakras in one continuous flow of energy. The interrelatedness of my chakras was palpable, especially in my crown,

heart, and sacral centers. I "saw" an inner light illuminating my
central channel, radiating out a soft, white glow like the light of
the moon.

Relax—that was her advice. It was very powerful. And Feminine.
It's a step I so often want to skip in my urgency to "get there"—
wherever "there" is. It's not easy for me to relax.

Figure 6-1. RELAXATION PRACTICE

RELAX!

SEVEN

Transparency

*M*ary contacted me again two days later to deliver her fourth transmission in our initial period of working together.

Blessings to you again, my dearest sister,

Now you are ready for the next step, which is the opening of your throat chakra. For you, this is specifically associated with the opening of your sacral chakra.

It takes willpower for you to use your voice and communicate when you are very open in your sacral center. This is a challenge for many women, while men tend to be naturally open in the throat chakra. It is the heart chakra and the vulnerable, open aspect of the sacral chakra that is more challenging for most men.

In actuality, the challenges at the various chakras can occur in various ways for men or women. It really depends upon how strong an individual is in the Masculine or Feminine within. But generally speaking, men follow the Masculine pattern and women follow the Feminine pattern.

To open your throat to honest expression, you will need to use the willpower of the solar plexus chakra. The easiest way to accomplish this is to have a structure through which you engage verbal expression. A structure will provide a framework for bringing in your will, without you having to generate it internally.

This is where Tantric practices can be extremely helpful. They create a form, which has always been a part of your spirituality—through practices, ritual, ceremony, etc. It is very useful to bring this same kind of structure and form into the context of your sexuality. This will elevate your sexuality to a higher level and support all your chakras being open, active, and harmonized.

Transparency is necessary for the full merging of two beings. You are to be completely open and be seen by each other all the way through to your divinity. This means that you are to bring your honest communication of all your feelings to your partner—all that may be disturbing you, all your questions, all that you need to reveal to be totally open and transparent. You both are to do this.

Many people are afraid to show themselves to their partner. It's somehow easier to open your body to another than to open your whole being and psyche. Yet this is necessary for the depth of union to occur. You must also be willing to receive your partner fully, even the parts that you react to. This, too, is part of intimacy. Otherwise you won't be fully present and available to each other.

What are you afraid to reveal to your partner—afraid that if you reveal it you won't be loved and accepted? What are you afraid to hear from your partner—afraid that if you hear that, it will mean you're not loved and accepted?

Often what you're afraid to reveal are emotions. You may have feelings of not liking things the other person has done. You may feel afraid to reveal attractions to others or to hear about your partner's attractions. You may feel insecure about things that you or your partner want to do with another person, or things another person wants to do with one of you.

Yet if you reveal these things to each other, you will be amazed at the depth of intimacy and rise in sexual energy it will activate between you. Conversely, if you don't reveal them, you will experience the results of your intimacy and sexual energy shutting down.

When you open fully with each other, you are then in a position to navigate the process of responding together to whatever you have shared. This, too, will create intimacy between you. What was before a challenge will now become a contribution to your greater connectedness and enhanced closeness with each other, thus deepening your intimacy. In general, the outcome will be different than what would have occurred if you had withheld from each other and acted in separation.

This is a radical idea for many of you, quite different from the way you were trained to relate to others. It requires trust, ultimately trust in God, that who you are is fine, just the way you are. There is nothing wrong with you that needs to be hidden. The same is true for your partner. Neither of you is doing anything wrong or bad.

Of course you will feel attraction for others—you are connected to others. If you bring this into your relationship, it can serve your intimacy and passion. Of course there will be things about the other that you do not like. If you bring this into your relationship, it will open your hearts to each other. And your hearts will lead you to a resolution.

Transparency is essential. Do not spend your intimate time in the superficialities of your mind, reporting the news of the day to each other or all the thoughts you're having at the superficial level of your ideas. Go deeper to what is at your center. That will support both of you. Everything you need is being given to you. You simply must connect with yourself and share it with your partner. Then you are sharing your God-connection with each other.

I love you and support you most fully.
I AM Mary Magdalene

*W*hile Mary's earlier message about connecting with my sacral chakra led me to communicate with people through my eyes, now she was asking me to activate my throat chakra to communicate verbally. She knew this was difficult for me. I don't have problems with verbal communication in most situations, but when I open up sexually my ability to speak to my partner seems to evaporate. It takes tremendous willpower for me to pry open my vocal chords in such situations. Mary's solution was to bring in a structure for verbal sharing in the midst of sexual occasions.

I was aware of several such structures. One was to use a "talking piece." In this practice, whoever is holding the object designated as the talking piece speaks while the other person listens from their heart without interrupting. The obvious disadvantage of using this technique in the context of intimacy is that it requires an external object, which may disrupt the flow of your occasion.

Another structure I was familiar with was time setting—identifying a specific period of time, such as three minutes, for each person to talk, then going back and forth as often as necessary until both people are complete. This, too, could be potentially awkward, as it involved timing each other and because both people may not require the same amount of time to speak.

The communication structure I favored most was a script-based technique I called "the sharing process." This approach involves memorizing a simple script and then using it to guide the verbal exchange. It goes like this:

Person A: "There's something I haven't shared with you."

Person B: "OK. Would you like to tell me?"

Person A: "Yes."

> Person A then proceeds to tell Person B whatever they wish to share, while Person B listens all the way to the end without interrupting.

Person B: "Thank you. Is there anything else?"

Person A: "Yes, there's something I haven't shared with you."

Person B: "OK. Would you like to tell me?"

Person A: "Yes."

> Person A then proceeds to tell Person B whatever they wish to share, while Person B listens all the way to the end without interrupting.

Person B: "Thank you. Is there anything else?"

The interchange continues until Person A feels complete, having expressed everything they want to share. Person A then says no in answer to the question "Is there anything else?" At that point, the partners switch roles and Person B begins sharing while Person A listens. The partners continue switching roles until both have shared everything they want to.

The point is to select information that is important to you to share with your partner, or things that you think your partner would want to know and might be upset if they later found out you hadn't communicated those things. I had engaged this technique with my previous partner. When we first began using it, I was terribly afraid that I would hear about him being endlessly attracted to other women and wouldn't be able to deal with it. My experience turned out to be surprisingly different. I found out that, in reality, he was rarely attracted to other women. Using this structure actually alleviated my fears, which had existed mostly in my imagination. I also discovered that when he did express an attraction to someone, I was able to stay calm and listen to his words rather than jump into a reaction that was blown far out of proportion to what he was expressing. The discipline of sticking to the script provided spaciousness for me to feel safe and thus respond from a much more balanced place.

Most of the time, we communicated information we hadn't gotten around to sharing simply because of our busy schedules.

Sometimes, we shared tender emotions, like feeling hurt or lonely or resentful. Always the sharing process helped us to vocalize our feelings in spite of any anxiety we may have felt, while also helping us to know that we were heard. This would then allow us to hear the other's response. Inevitably, difficulties would be resolved so much more easily than we had expected. More importantly, we would be unburdened of our emotional baggage and returned to a state of heart connection with each other. An added bonus was that this would invariably lead to great sex. We used to laugh about how this technique was the only foreplay we needed.

Now it was time to inaugurate this practice with Tony. I imagined it would help me stay real in our relationship rather than drift off into a fantasy of wishful thinking and later crash when confronted with reality. I also suspected that expressing my honest feelings would help bring in my Masculine side of caring for myself by making choices that would treat my heart well.

Figure 7-1. TRANSPARENCY PRACTICE

Open your throat chakra to honest expression with your partner.
Use a structure to support you.

Figure 7-2. THE SHARING PROCESS

Contributed by Mercedes Kirkel

1. Follow this script with your partner:

   Person A: "There's something I haven't shared with you."

   Person B: "OK. Would you like to tell me?"

   Person A: "Yes."

   Person A then proceeds to tell Person B whatever they wish to share, while Person B listens all the way to the end without interrupting.

   Person B: "Thank you. Is there anything else?"

2. Repeat step 1 until Person A feels complete, having expressed everything they want to share. Person A then responds no in answer to the question "Is there anything else?" At that point, the partners switch roles and Person B begins sharing while Person A listens.

3. Continue switching roles until you have both shared everything you want to.

EIGHT

Resonance

*O*n an early September morning, a little over two weeks after her initial communication, Mary continued her sequence of instructions.

Blessings to you, dear one,

We are ready for me to show you more. But first let us return to the Sea of Galilee, for you have been through much and such a purification will return you to your open heart-and-body space. So take my hand, dearest sister, and come with me. Enter the sea as we walk upon the waves. Feel yourself lifted by the swells and gently lowered. Feel the sun on your face, the wind in your hair, like the gentle breath of the Goddess caressing you. Let your body soften and be carried. With this, you can add the opening of your heart, sacral, and root chakra, in the way you have been practicing and becoming strong. Breathe in deeply, and feel the light energy fill you with freshness and life. That is good. Now we are ready to begin.

I feel so much love for you. I want to affirm this, so that you know it fully. This love is personal to you, and you can receive it personally. It is also universal, the love of our Father-Mother-God. But that does not make it impersonal. This is important to know. Some of the people in your spiritual world today have become confused, thinking that love in its universal form is impersonal. It can be in certain circumstances, but it is often simultaneously personal. The Father-God love is imper-

sonal; the Mother-God love is personal. And the union of the two is both personal and impersonal. This is important to understand. It is part of the sacred union that you are entering into.

Your love with your partner is both personal and impersonal. You are loving that person in very particular and specific ways that are personal to that individual. But this love also has an impersonal quality as it is a reflection, a distillation, of universal love. Consequently your radiation and emanation of love out to all others is increased, energized, and strengthened. Experiencing love with a partner, both personal and impersonal, is part of entering into divine union with them.

Let us review the steps we've covered so far. You have worked to open your heart, sacral, and root chakras. Then you brought in the element of relaxing, allowing, opening. Next you used your throat and solar plexus chakras to express to your partner whatever required expressing, especially relative to emotions and sexuality. The resulting transparency created an open channel of vulnerability, bonding you deeply with your partner and releasing any blocked energy between you.

Now you are ready for your next step, which is to bring your chakras into a frequency of resonance with your partner. There are various ways to do this. I recommend beginning with the heart. Using breath and intention, breathe together for several breaths to harmonize the frequencies of the heart. Next, repeat this procedure at the solar plexus chakra, the sacral chakra, then the root chakra. Then return to your heart and once again harmonize with your partner. Now harmonize the frequencies at your throat, third eye, and crown chakras, then return once again to your heart. Try the sequence now with yourself.

Often one partner breathes more slowly than the other. Synchronizing your breathing brings these frequencies into resonance, thereby laying a platform for your subtler energies to then harmonize.

Going to your solar plexus chakra (your power center) before the sacral and root chakras creates a state of safety in which to open those more tender chakras. When you harmonize your solar plexus chakra first, you relieve the sacral chakra of the burden of being confused and intermingled with power, allowing it to be in its pure, vulnerable state.

The root chakra is also quite vulnerable because it is involved with physicality and survival. Again with this chakra, you've created the safety of first harmonizing the frequencies of your power center at the solar plexus. Then you can harmonize and open your root chakra in vulnerability and purity.

With the return to your heart chakra, you are melding the energy of the first four chakras so that they are aligned, harmonized, strong, and integrated both internally and with respect to your partner's first four chakras. This forms a strong platform for energizing and harmonizing the higher chakras.

Can you feel the sweetness of opening your throat chakra? It is like releasing a song—your soul song—which can then harmonize with the soul song of your partner. This is most important. The closest you may have come to this in the past was while listening to the sounds of the dolphins or whales communicating with each other. There is much, even most, that you cannot hear with your human ears. But this gives you a sense.

Now as you energize and harmonize your third eye chakra, you will be taken into your depths, opened up to the greater cosmos, and aligned to your place within it. This, too, is most powerful to do in tandem with another. In harmonizing your third eye chakra with your partner's you are forming a great cosmic bond with your partner, which carries a frequency into the cosmos that continues through time and space. It also makes you available for greater cosmic gifts and experiences.

The crown chakra is the bridge to higher dimensions. It opens the doorway for your loving to transport you to higher dimensions, uniting your consciousness and manifestation with those dimensions. Again, energizing and harmonizing this chakra with a partner's strengthens the outcome for both of you.

Finally, you return for a third time to your heart, which integrates all the chakras you have opened, energized, and harmonized, below and *above. This is a good time to consciously connect with all your chakras and feel the merging with your partner's chakras. Working with the higher chakras is so ecstatic that many people want to stay connected to them. It can take intention to bring forth the lower three chakras in balance with the higher ones. It is easily done, though, if you put your attention on it.*

This is a most beautiful and intimate practice. I know you will greatly enjoy it. I urge you to practice it and allow its full pleasure to be experienced. It will also slow you down into cosmic time and pacing. This, too, is part of the process.

I love you, dear one, and bless you, yet again, with all my heart.
I AM Mary Magdalene

Two nights earlier, Tony had come over spontaneously in response to a text I sent him about the magnificent harvest moon that was rising. We sat on my front porch and watched the moon for about an hour. Then we said good night. Our time together was simple, sweet, and beautiful.

The following night, after going to a birthday party for Tony's friend at a lovely restaurant, we came back to my house. We put on a CD we'd purchased at the party, then I read Tony the first of Mary's transmissions. He enjoyed hearing it. Following Mary's instruction, he began practicing opening up his heart, sacral, and root chakras. We immediately felt our love and passion for each other coming to life.

I could tell this was a time to follow Mary's more recent instruction of communicating information that was important for me to express, so I took a big breath and began.

First I talked about what I needed in order to renew our sexual relationship. I told Tony, "I've realized I need to see you more regularly. My preference is to see you every day, but I could handle every other day if we talked on the phone on the in-between days we didn't see each other." Aware that Tony's arc of feeling moved to spend time together was much longer than mine, I knew I was asking for a change.

"I also want us to agree to be monogamous," I continued. This was something we'd never explicitly discussed. When we'd been together in the past, I'd never heard him talk about anyone else. But now, to be sure there would be no one else, I wanted to make a conscious commitment to monogamy.

"The third thing I need is to know we both want the same thing for our future. My desire is to eventually live together and get married. I'm not sure what your desire is, and I'd like to know." I sensed this might be the biggest stumbling block for us. Nevertheless, I needed resolution in all three of these areas to give me a container of emotional safety if I was going to open myself sexually with him again.

There was also something else I needed to discuss, which felt more challenging. During the time we'd been separated, I'd had a brief involvement with another man. Although I no longer felt any draw to him, I wanted Tony to know this had occurred so I could feel completely open with him again.

Tony took this news hard. "I feel jealous hearing that you were with another man," he said. "I don't like the emotions I'm having." Experiencing Tony this way was new for me. Generally he was extremely even tempered, his energy and emotions consistently upbeat. Not knowing where this conversation would lead us, I felt apprehensive. All I knew was that I wanted to keep talking, trusting that we'd be led to whatever was best for both of us.

We continued with the sharing process. When it was my turn, I mirrored Tony's feelings back to him. He was then able to delve further into what was coming up for him. As he continued to express his feelings, the charge he had felt started to dissipate. He acknowledged, "You didn't do anything 'wrong' because we weren't together at that point." He seemed to be talking through his thoughts and feelings. I watched in wonder and relief as he found his way back to peace.

Once we'd shared everything, our attraction suddenly ballooned forward. It was hard for us to not to be sexual. We both felt our desire very strongly. Two times we nearly went ahead, but I stopped

Figure 8-1. CHAKRA

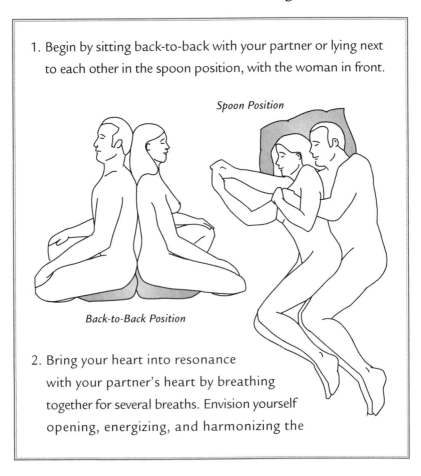

1. Begin by sitting back-to-back with your partner or lying next to each other in the spoon position, with the woman in front.

Spoon Position

Back-to-Back Position

2. Bring your heart into resonance with your partner's heart by breathing together for several breaths. Envision yourself opening, energizing, and harmonizing the

us. This was quite different for me and not at all easy. But I felt a newfound strength and ability to do so from the clarity I had received through our verbal sharing.

At the end of the night we agreed that we'd talk about what we both wanted for ourselves and with each other, and how we would like to proceed. Even though it was challenging to restrain our mutual impulse to "go for it," it felt good to feel so open and desirous of each other. I was glad we were bringing more consciousness to our choice of whether to engage sexually together.

RESONANCE PRACTICE

frequencies of your heart with your partner's heart. Allow your breathing to come into synchronicity with your partner's breathing.

3. Repeat step 2 at the solar plexus, then the sacral and root chakras.

4. Returning to the heart chakra, open, energize, and harmonize frequencies with your partner through breathing and intention, as you continue to integrate the frequencies of your solar plexus, sacral, and root chakras.

5. Proceed to open, energize, and harmonize frequencies with your partner at the throat, third eye, then crown chakras.

6. Return to the heart chakra a third time, repeating the same process of harmonizing with your partner at the heart through breathing and intention. Then connect with all of your chakras and feel the merging with all of your partner's chakras. If necessary, use your intention to bring the lower three chakras into balance with the higher chakras.

NINE

The Beauty of Emotions

*A*fter Tony left, I checked my email. To my surprise, the man I'd been briefly connected with had written to me. Though his email was short and positive, it triggered painful memories for me of emotional issues that were unresolved between us. I woke up the next morning still feeling disturbed by his communication. Mary picked up on my agitated state right away in her message to me that morning.

Blessings, my dear one,

You are feeling very complicated this morning in your reaction to the email you received last night. This is because you doubt yourself and have difficulty owning your emotions. You do not see your emotions as beautiful or a gift to others. You doubt that others will care about your feelings or will love you if you express them. This is because you don't tend to care about your feelings and love yourself for them.

This is a deep area for you, one that causes you many problems. You bring your emotional complications to others, and their responses reflect your complications. This self-fulfilling prophecy is one of the ways in which you create your reality, including the responses you receive from others. This is a big factor in your life because you are a very emotional person.

Being highly emotional is truly one of your strengths, but you do not yet realize this. You were trained to think of your emotional nature as a weakness and a burden to others. And because you are acting as though your emotions are still an unwelcome hardship for others, they actually are a burden to others.

Most people are not as emotionally sensitive and open as you are, so they don't understand what you are going through. Those who are emotionally sensitive have generally received the same suppressive training as you. So they're struggling with their personal prison of suppression and are lost in their own confusion and darkness when they respond to you. Since they don't have clarity about their own emotions, they cannot have clarity about yours—especially when yours are still masked by your suppression.

Because of your emotional sensitivity and your level of consciousness, you have the ability to help others understand emotions, become more emotionally sensitive, and heal from their emotional suppression. In fact, you are meant be a leader in this healing modality. But first, you must shift your perception from burdening others with your emotions into feeding them with your emotions.

Emotions are packets of life energy that nourish others, much like sexuality and other forms of energy feed people. In fact, emotions and sexuality are closely related. Both run on the same frequency, and you must be emotionally open to experience and convey the fullness of sex, including bonding at the heart.

Communicating about sexuality creates a vehicle for emotional sharing to happen in a positive and healthy way. You are making progress in this area. It was good when you made a joke the other day and said, "We need to have our talk soon," as you felt your passion and desire arising with Tony. Your talk with him yesterday, where you explained what you need in order to reengage with him sexually, as well as telling him about your involvement with someone else while the two of you weren't together, were very good steps for you. They supported you in maintaining your commitment to wait to enter into a sexual relationship with Tony, even in the midst of feeling your longing and desire for each other.

You must hold to this practice of communicating your emotions. You know how to communicate in a responsible manner, without blame or judgment. But you are still not loving your emotions fully enough, which is why your communication tends to be unclear and complicated.

How would you communicate if you were absolutely clear that your emotions were beautiful and a gift to yourself and others? What if you were connected to your emotions all the time and able to communicate from that place, as though sharing a beautiful experience with another? What if you were absolutely sure this was a contribution to the other even if they didn't necessarily express that in their response, just as you're sure that your spiritual insights and guidance are a gift to others?

This is what you must shift into. It will make a huge difference. You are very confident in your sexuality and are totally sure your sexuality is a valuable gift to others; you must come to feel the same way about your emotions. Then others will reflect this disposition back to you and your experiences will be very different. Others will respect you for your emotional expression, will look to you for guidance in this area, and will trust you relative to emotions. This shift can happen relatively quickly because you already have the skills. All you need is an adjustment into valuing your emotions.

I am supporting you and blessing you to make this adjustment, to enter into the wonderful space of loving your emotions. It will open up a magnificent world for you. This is your next lesson and focus of work.

In love and blessing,
I AM Mary Magdalene

Figure 9-1.
COMMUNICATING THE BEAUTY OF EMOTIONS

1. Accept your emotions as beautiful gifts to yourself and others.

2. Communicate your emotions clearly to others.

TEN

God-Goddess Kiss

*T*he following night I read Tony all of Mary's transmissions that had come in since the first one. He was very attentive and involved, and then replied, "Thank you for sharing these transmissions with me. I've been using Mary's first instruction of connecting the heart, sacral, and root chakras. I added in connecting to the throat chakra as soon as I heard about it. All these practices are very simple. And I can feel them making a difference in our relationship already.

"I'm grateful that she gave these instructions to you. I'd like to read them daily, just to remind myself. I think if we create a regular practice of this, it will become second nature. With the initial practice, I discovered that the connection with my sacral chakra became ongoing. I found myself doing the practice even when I wasn't thinking about it—like while I was working or driving. I just realized I was doing it. It's like a walking meditation. You can do it as you go about your day."

I asked him, "What did you experience when you did that first practice?"

He responded, "The first time we did the practice in your office, right after we read Mary's instructions, I experienced different colored lights and pictures, too. I thought that was very strange and wondered where those pictures were coming from. Then later she mentioned that we might have images or light come up during the practices.

"I think everybody should be doing this beautiful practice. It could change the way people relate to each other altogether. I'm seeing it as a stepping-stone into the fourth dimension. So please thank Mary for me."

Then I asked him, "Do you sense Mary's presence while engaging this practice?"

"Oh yes. I've been feeling her since you first starting talking about her. Hearing her transmissions and things you've shared makes me feel like I've always known her. I think I have a deep connection to her from two thousand years ago. I think I knew her. I feel a deep love for her."

Hearing Tony say he thought he knew Mary from two thousand years ago pushed my doubt button. It had taken me a long time to come to realize that I knew Mary from two thousand years ago, even after exploring memories and other information that had validated my history with her. I didn't have any problem with the idea that I knew Tony in one or more past lives. Being guided to the church where we met almost immediately after my arrival in Santa Fe, the way we seemed to recognize each other so readily, the ease with which we seemed to relate to each other, and the similarity of our values and spiritual paths all pointed to having known each other in previous lives. And while I could easily imagine that one of these lives may have been within the Essene community, I still felt skeptical when Tony said he knew Mary personally. *Is he extrapolating from my experiences,* I wondered, *or are these his own memories and intuitions?*

I quickly saw the cosmic humor in doubting Tony's claim to have known Mary, as I was sure many people had the same doubts about me. *Ultimately,* I told myself, *what difference does it make? Tony*

*is who he is now, and I have no questions about that, no doubt about the
beauty of who he is and the gifts he brings. That's all that really matters.*

Returning to our conversation, I probed Tony further about his
experiences: "Do you have a sense of trust in what Mary's saying
about sexuality?"

"Yes, definitely. I have no trouble with that at all. In fact, I think
we've known these things all along and just forgotten them. So, yes,
I trust her implicitly. And already I see the differences her transmissions are making in my life."

"Can you say what those differences are?" I asked.

"One difference is that I feel more closeness with God. There's
a constant connection. I feel it not only when I meditate but even
during my sleep. I wake up in the middle of the night and talk to
him. It's like he's there all the time. I thought I only could connect
with God at certain times. Now I realize we need to live connected
to him all the time.

"Something else that's different for me is the element of transparency, being able to express everything to each other. Now I'm
not afraid to show you any part of myself.

"Another difference is something I observed while we were at
the restaurant tonight. We were sitting side by side as we usually
do, touching and kissing and eating and talking when I noticed, out
of the corner of my eye, that a woman at another table was watching
us. At first I thought it was because she was uncomfortable with
our public display of affection. But after hearing Mary's transmissions
tonight, I think people look at us because we're relating in the fourth
dimension and they're seeing that. They're seeing us reveal who we
really are and are experiencing what the fourth dimension looks like
through our relating."

At that point, we stopped talking and started kissing. It was slow
and deeply sensual. I felt transported, reminding me of a very special

experience I'd had a year before in Sedona. I was at a workshop where the participants had taken part in a group spirit-journey, traveling in our light bodies into the center of the Earth. There I met two very loving and wise fourth-dimensional beings who gave me powerful and insightful experiences. Near the end of my journey, I made love with the beings in their fourth-dimensional way and emerged deeply changed. I thought I had experienced fourth- or fifth-dimensional lovemaking in my previous experiences with Tantra, but this journey showed me that fourth-dimensional intimacy was much more than I'd ever imagined.

What was happening now with Tony wasn't the full experience I'd had with those beings, but it was reminiscent of it. Tony was feeling it, too. He told me, "I'm seeing lots of beautiful colors that I don't usually see." I saw them as well, especially a yellow-goldish hue that was really a swirl of colors forming a large, horizontal oval around our midsections. The oval was in the shape of the *merkaba*, which looks like a flying saucer.[1] We were merging our light bodies, becoming one light body.

Tony said, "I'm hearing a very high-pitched sound. It isn't coming from my ears. It's coming from my heart."

I responded by saying, "Part of my daily meditation is to go into what I call the inner temple of my heart. When I do that, I hear frequencies that I specifically associate with that sacred space. I think we're connecting those parts of our hearts."

"This feels very familiar," Tony replied. "I remember having done this with you before—not in this lifetime, but a previous one."

We kept kissing. Whenever I felt self-conscious or started thinking, I would remember the practice of opening the heart, sacral, and root chakras. That would instantly shift me into a seamless flow of connected energy once again. I felt the Goddess coming into me, filling me and animating me. Tony asked what was happening and I said, "We're manifesting God-Goddess energy."

"Yes," he replied.

Our intimacy was slow, deep, and smooth, drawing us in more and more. And we were only kissing! I let go into his manliness, and it felt natural and good to give myself to him. We continued embracing and kissing, becoming melded together in an exquisite God-Goddess kiss.

ELEVEN

Letting Go

*T*wo days later I received a new message from Mary in my early morning meditation.

Dear one,

You are running yourself down by trying to catch up with all your work. You need to relax and let go. Trust God and the universe to accomplish what needs accomplishing. Yes, you need to do your part, but that is not your challenge. Your challenge is to remain balanced and let go.

The universe has intervened in your life, taking you on a different course from what you were anticipating. You must allow this and learn to flow with it through feeling and the opening of your sacral chakra that you have been practicing. Make that practice your priority. Put it first, before all your functioning. Give it space and attention consistently. Then add other functions as directed by your higher self, your balanced self. This realignment of your way of relating to life will keep you connected to God, your higher self, and life itself. Then everything you do will be blessed and empowered and appropriate.

This is a trying time for you. You seem to have been given more to do than is possible; do not try to accomplish it from your will and physical functioning. Instead, connect with God and act from your higher self. Then all is possible.

*And do not forget pleasure, joy, and relaxation. It is good that
you are dancing, for that feeds you in many ways. You must also stay
connected to nature and do things that are relaxing.*

I love you and believe in you fully.

With all my blessings,
I AM Mary Magdalene

*M*ary's message seemed to be preparing me for the difficulty of
the day. Already I was feeling disturbed by a strange energy. Upon
beginning my work, I realized how backlogged I'd become, having
spent the last two and a half weeks helping my parents.

In the late morning I went to a doctor's appointment. An aide
there who was extremely serving and kind told me twice that I
had a beautiful smile. I didn't feel at all beautiful that morning,
but this model of simplicity and devotion helped pull me out of
my funk.

In the afternoon Tony came over and we continued our talk
from the night before, when we had briefly discussed reengaging
our sexual relationship. We used the sharing process, and I went
first. "I want to get clarity on how you feel about what I said I need
in our relationship—seeing you regularly, being monogamous, and
planning our future together."

Tony replied, "I'm still processing what happened in my last
relationship. I want to understand why I allowed myself to marry
someone I didn't love." This was a "lightbulb moment" for me. I
thought Tony had loved his wife initially and that his feelings
had changed over time. But now I was hearing that even in the
beginning he hadn't loved her. Suddenly his reluctance to make a
commitment to me made a lot more sense. He'd lost trust in himself,

fearing he would repeat the same pattern and end up in a loveless relationship.

My heart opened in compassion for him, even as I understood that he couldn't give me what I wanted, at least not now. The path ahead suddenly became crystal clear, and before I knew what was happening, words came tumbling out of my mouth: "I need to let go of being in relationship with you." Tony was seeing the same thing.

It all seemed obvious and natural, even if it wasn't what we wished were happening. We said good-bye, and I felt the realness of it. Yet inside I had a strong feeling of peace and clarity.

The next few days were like slogging through sadness. Thankfully, working, spending time with a friend, and going to my Argentine tango class all helped me to get through. By day three my energy had returned and I enjoyed a productive morning. Tony came over in the afternoon so we could return items we each had that belonged to the other. To my amazement, our time together felt simple and easy. I went out dancing that night, pleasantly surprised that I could feel so good.

TWELVE

Feeding Intimacy

My next communication from Mary came two days later.

Blessings, my dear one,

I am happy to be communicating again and to have this time together. Do not be concerned about feeling that you have been away for a long time. You have had much to attend to, as well as caring for yourself in the midst of it all. It is true that your sense of separation during this time has affected your level of connection with me and our communication. This is natural.

The sense of separation is inherent in the third dimension. You could say that separation is the default position, the place a person keeps returning to until they create a different experience for themselves through intention and consciousness. This is what spiritual practice does. Using intention and discipline, it becomes possible to cultivate a higher level of consciousness to reside in regardless of the outer or inner events of your life. However, if lapses in your practice become too long, over time you may lose the capacity to transcend the third dimension.

This is what has happened to you. Major life events—such as caring for your father and stepmother, falling behind in your work activities, and ending your relationship with Tony—have taken their toll on you. As a result, your instincts are telling you to function physically and your mind is telling you to attend to all the practical details of life. However, the more you allow your higher self to put your spiritual practice first, the more the other areas of your life, including the physical and practical, will fall into place with grace and efficacy. This takes what you call faith because you are operating from a higher level than the arena in which events are pulling on your attention.

So you have slipped somewhat. That is part of your human experience. Forgive yourself. Understand what happened, and return to your practice of strengthening your higher connections. Learn from what occurred so that you make better choices in the future. And understand that you made the choices you did for real reasons. You were choosing to care for your loved ones, to sustain your work life and book promotion, and to support yourself emotionally during the painful loss of your relationship with Tony. These were all ways of attending to your inner divine qualities.[1] See it as such, rather than a failure on your part. See how you could have strengthened those efforts by making your spiritual practice a priority. Then all that you've done becomes a beautiful process of growing in light.

Even though you are not currently in a relationship and able to engage my instruction with a partner, there is no problem with continuing our work together—I can still communicate all that you need to know and practice. And you may have a partner to practice with sooner than you are currently aware of. So I am happy to continue.

I will review what we have done so far, as part of our reconnecting and refocusing. We began with opening your heart, sacral, and root chakras through intention, visualization, and feeling. As the energy started moving through the chakras and your whole self, we deepened the process through relaxation. This made you receptive to the kundalini flow. Then we focused on opening your throat chakra through communication and supporting that with your will through your solar plexus chakra.

As we discussed before, communication is a challenging area for you, even though your communication skills are strong. You tend to hide your emotions, because of your fears that others don't care about your feelings. When you try to break out of this hiding, you become very complicated and bring a lot of emotional anxiety into your communications. As a result, your communications tend to be difficult and often don't result in your being understood or having the outcomes you would like.

The solution to all this is to work through your emotional reactivity before communicating. It will take extra work on your part at this stage but will help you achieve positive experiences in your communications. It will also help heal and transform the pattern you have that is complicating your communications.

Difficulties especially arise for you when you express something another person is doing that you're not enjoying and would like to change. First you must become clear that there's nothing wrong with what you're feeling. What you're feeling is a gift, often due to your heightened sensitivity, especially with regard to energy, emotion, and intellectual understanding.

When you come to accept your responses and feelings, you will also experience compassion for the others involved. Often they're doing what they're doing out of some kind of emotional stress. But you don't tend to see that because you're consumed by your own emotional reaction. Once you attend to your own fear, hurt, or sadness, you are then free to tune in to the other person's reality and understand what is motivating them. This will naturally lead you to feel compassion for their challenges.

From there, you can choose how to communicate. The more you make the communication about yourself and your feelings, the easier it will be for the other person to hear what you're saying. Help the other person to understand your feelings and your challenges. This will inspire their compassion for you. It will also provide safety for them to be vulnerable, opening the door for them to share their feelings and challenges with you. This will lead to intimacy.

You have seen that it truly does work this way. You just get blocked in the early stages at times because of your negative self-perceptions and defensive patterns. This is already in the process of healing and will continue to do so as you continue to engage this process I am describing.

Your sensitivity is a gift, but also a responsibility that requires more of you. You must help others understand you and meet you with equal sensitivity on their part. This will require patience and a bit more skill on your part. You must maintain your Feminine role while offering help and even instruction. The more you make it about you and leave the other person entirely out of it, other than asking for their support for what you need, the better this will work.

Women are the leaders in communicating about emotions and energies they're experiencing. Men can also lead, but it is not as natural for them. Men must learn to trust women to lead in this way. And women must learn to lead in a way that's safe for men, where they're not criticizing them or complaining. This is a great shift for many in your world.

Men love to give to women, as long as they're not being criticized or told how to help. Simply make it clear what you need help with, then give them space to decide how to assist you. This wonderful play feeds the intimacy between a man and a woman.

I love you and bless you and shine the light of love upon you.
I AM Mary Magdalene

THIRTEEN

Following the Stream of Energy

*M*ary continued her instruction with this message two days later.

Blessings to you again, my dear sister,

You have laid the groundwork for opening and connecting with your self and a partner—opening your chakras, connecting with your partner through speech, and energetically connecting with your partner's chakras. At this point your energy body, also known as your etheric body, is open and activated. You are attuned etherically to yourself and your partner.

This is a delicious state to be enjoyed. It may feel like you're being carried by energy, as if floating downstream in a river. You will probably have a sense of relaxing your everyday functioning modes, including your thinking. If you're not experiencing this, it is a sign that there is an emotional issue that still needs tending to. In that case, you would probably want to return to the verbal-exchange practice to connect with your emotions and reveal them to your partner. Through that process, either the emotions will release or you will know how to attend to them.

Now you are ready to engage your partner physically, which includes all the intimate ways in which humans are drawn to each other, such as kissing, touching, holding, and embracing. This stage is commonly referred to in your world as foreplay. I do not find that to be the best

83

term because it implies that it's of less importance than what follows. This has the effect of orienting the partners toward a future goal rather than allowing them to be fully in the present and allowing the interchange to organically unfold. This aspect of being fully in the present— of coming completely into the current moment as an energetic experience—is an essential component of sacred sexuality.

During this initial phase of physical connection, there are several things to be aware of. The first is that the slower you go in engaging each other, the fuller and richer your experience will be. This is something like enjoying a fine wine, where, rather than gulping it down to get to the meal, you want to fully experience it through all your senses. So it is with your physical connection. You may be surprised to discover how much more there is to experience when you slow things down and how much it expands and increases the pleasure of your engagement.

What will support you in coming into the present is to breathe fully and deeply. Many people have the tendency to hold their breath or breathe shallowly when they're excited. In sacred sexuality, you want to do just the opposite, allowing your breath to naturally slow down. This will help you in maintaining a slower speed in your engagement. It will also allow you to feel and experience at a much greater depth and fullness. Your breath is a powerful medium for opening you to deeper states—a fact known to practitioners of meditation, the yogic practice of pranayama, or other forms of breathwork.[1] Similarly, in sexuality the breath is a vital medium of going deeper, carrying you to new regions, terrains, and vistas of beingness.

Along with this, also be aware of your touch and the pressure you bring to it. Light pressure tends to support energetic connection, whereas heavier pressure may override the sense of connecting with energy. You will generally find that a light touch is most effective in stimulating and playing with energy, which is what you are doing at this stage.

Sense how the energy is calling to you and wants you to move. In some ways, it is like working with a Ouija board and discovering that the energy has its own movement that can carry you and direct your touch.[2] Remain sensitive to the stream of energy passing through you, and let it carry you to your deepest currents of feeling, response, and openness.

Blessings, dear one, as we travel this path together.
I AM Mary Magdalene

Figure 13-1. INITIATING PHYSICAL CONNECTION

1. Begin to engage your partner physically, including kissing, touching, holding, and embracing.

2. Staying fully in the present, allow what's happening in the current moment to guide you.

3. Slow down to fully experience what's happening.

4. Breathe fully and deeply.

5. Use a light touch to support your energetic connection with your partner.

6. Be aware of the movement of energy, and let your physical movements follow the energy flow.

FOURTEEN

Chakra Bliss

The following morning, Tony sent me a text, saying, "I've been missing you and I'm feeling sad. I send you my love." I was surprised to receive this. We'd been apart for a week, and I'd been keeping busy with my life and enjoying what I was doing. Unlike Tony, I wasn't feeling sad about not being together.

I texted him back: "Thank you for sharing your feelings. I send you love, too." But our interchange started me thinking about him. In the afternoon I went hiking in the mountains outside of Santa Fe with a good friend. As we drove up the road to the ski area, I pointed out places where Tony and I had enjoyed special times together: the spot we had picnicked on Easter, the overlook where we'd viewed the solar eclipse, the trail where we'd hiked on the solstice. When I returned home, I realized how much his communication had affected me. I sent him another text: "I'm missing you, too."

His response was quick and decisive: "Want to go out to lunch tomorrow?"

I called him back, and we had a warm, heart-connecting talk, bubbling over with all the things we wanted to share with each other. At one point I asked him, "Are you asking me out on a date?"

"Yes," he said.

I immediately responded, "I'd love that!"

Our lunch date was wonderful. Tony looked so handsome when he showed up, wearing an attractive Western shirt, ornate silver-buckled belt, and tight black pants. I'd put energy into looking extra nice, too, which he immediately noticed and complimented me on. Our yummy kisses made it obvious how happy we both were to be together. We had a delicious lunch at my favorite natural foods restaurant, sitting next to each other and catching up, feeling the attraction and joy flowing between us.

As we finished our last bites of lunch, Tony looked at me and said, "I've decided I want to be partners. I want you in my life. I want to share and create life together." I could hardly believe I was hearing those words and was all too happy to accept them as true.

On the drive back to my house, we passed a sales lot for RVs and Tony said, "Sometime soon let's go shopping for an RV. We've talked about traveling together and that would make it so easy." I was already seeing the adventures in my mind, enjoying future trips together.

I was taking it all in, feeling filled with delight. It seemed like my hopes were finally manifesting. As we pulled into my driveway, I said, "I need someone to practice Mary's instructions with. Would you like to do that with me?" His face lit up, and it was obvious he was as excited about doing that as I was. "Good," I said. "Let's go inside and try her most recent instruction of harmonizing our chakras."

We read the transmission together at my computer. Then we moved into the bedroom, preparing to engage the exercise by lying down on the bed in the spoon position (on our right sides, with me in front of Tony).

It was so good to feel Tony's body again. Even fully clothed, the energy between us was palpable. Yet the joy I experienced in our physical contact was quickly subsumed by a wave of sadness at not having been connected for so long. I realized I wasn't ready to engage Mary's practice. I needed some space to feel the sadness. I told Tony, "I want to do the sharing process." He readily agreed.

"I need to be really clear about what we're agreeing to," I began. "I know we've talked about this before, but I have to be sure I'm understanding what you're wanting now. Are you saying that you want to do what I want—seeing each other every day, or at the outside every other day, and talking in between; being monogamous; and having the intention to live together if we continue to feel good with each other?"

Tony said, "I want all that, including getting married in the future—although I don't want a church wedding, and maybe not even with a judge." I felt a reaction come up to the "not a judge" part, but I consciously chose not to focus on that, opting instead to fully receive how much we were in agreement on what we wanted.

This was new for me. I felt willing to commit to him with the intention of working to resolve our differences rather than holding out until our relationship seemed "perfect," or blaming Tony for not being "right." What seemed most important was having the opportunity to give and receive love. I felt like I was being offered a tremendous gift.

I noticed, and was celebrating, my growing ability to communicate about tough topics—subjects such as discussing our future, where I'd previously been afraid my partner wouldn't accept me or wouldn't want what I wanted—afraid that the discussion might lead to conflict or separation. I was using my gradually increasing strength in my Divine Masculine side to "do it anyway" by communicating my truth, even though it felt challenging to do so.

In a very short time everything had been expressed, and I felt myself come to peace. Now I was ready to engage Mary's practice. Returning to the spooning position, we began by merging our heart chakras. We did this for quite a while, which felt very profound. Tony put his hand on my heart, as we breathed together. I had the clear image of golden light coming from our hearts, along with somewhat hazy golden geometric shapes.

Then we moved to our solar plexus chakras. I felt myself surrendering my power to Tony in a deeper way than I think I'd ever felt. It was delicious and I felt so attracted to him as a man. I had the thought that this was a true union we were experiencing. Sparks of energy began to be released between us, like electric sparks. The visions and geometric shapes continued.

We proceeded to harmonize our sacral chakras and began having synchronous orgasms, our bodies moving together in rhythmic waves of undulation. This increased and intensified at the root chakra. I remember seeing beautiful, deep-blue colors and formations, which somewhat surprised me as I associate the root chakra with the color red. I think of dark blue as connected with the third eye chakra. I had the thought that, through our practice, the frequency of the root chakra was being lifted up to an entirely new vibration.

As we returned to our heart chakras, the orgasmic undulations continued, now incorporating all of our first four chakras. It was quite powerful.

Upon moving to the throat chakra, all movement ceased. I had the sense of releasing and merging our soul songs, just as Mary had described. It was like announcing our presence to the universe and finding our place, together.

As we connected our third eye chakras, I had a clear vision of very bright light emanating from a point in front of my third eye. Our orgasmic movements resumed, and I had a sense of traveling at great speed through the cosmos.

At our crown chakras, we once again became still. It felt like an active suspension, tuned to the gateway of the higher dimensions, like ecstatic stillness and peace.

Returning to the heart chakra a third time, we rested in the fullness of the merging of all our chakras.

Throughout the exercise, Tony rested his left hand on each of my chakras as we activated it. At the time that felt right to me, I moved his hand to the next chakra. At the third eye chakra, he also touched his third eye to the back of my head, which felt very powerful.

We were both amazed at what had happened. We started to move into physically expressing our love and attraction, kissing and embracing each other. Then Tony said, "I want you."

"I want you, too," I responded. But even as I said it, I could feel my hesitancy. Everything was happening so fast. I wanted to be sure I had the safety I needed to open myself up to him again. "Are you really ready to be in a committed relationship with me?" I asked. I marveled at the openness I was experiencing in my throat chakra, grateful for my newfound ability to express myself in a challenging moment with relative ease.

"Yes, I am," Tony affirmed. And with that we slid into making love.

It felt wonderful to be connecting fully again. Yet I noticed I still wasn't completely open. I could tell I had more healing to do from our separation. I suspected my reserve went even deeper than our recent split up or even our relationship altogether. I was touching into my long-standing pattern of distrust of relationships and men.

What I did trust was that I would be given whatever healing I needed, naturally and easily, in perfect timing.

FIFTEEN

Opening to Love and God

*T*hree days later I received Mary's next message.

Hello once more, my dear sister,

You are seeing how it is not necessary for you to "make" things happen relative to this work. That is most important, along with feeding yourself spiritually. The world works in such a different way than you understand with your mind. When you follow your mind, it leads to stress and a great deal of wasted energy and effort. The heart path is much more direct, clear, purposeful, and efficacious. Stay true to the heart path and let your guidance come from your heart, for then you will be doing what is best for you and all.

You are now ready to engage your partner physically. Of course, you want the physical environment to be prepared so that it is beautiful and honoring of the Goddess. This includes having the space clean and pleasing to the senses. You want it to be supportive of relaxation and dropping into your sensual nature. Make the space attractive, which may include lighting, artwork, a beautiful and comfortable bed and bedding, sensual music, flowers, and so forth. You can bring the sacred into the space through candles, incense, sacred pictures or music, and blessing the space beforehand. Be sure the temperature is comfortable, and have water available to drink.

You also want to prepare your bodies physically, so that your body is clean and attractive. You want your body and your breath to be washed and smelling good, and your hair to be attractive. It is good to wear attractive clothing that is sensual and also comfortable.

You want to be in a relaxed state, where your body is serene and you do not have other things on your mind. Turn off phones and other electronic devices so you will not be disturbed. If you have any responsibilities that need handling, including children, arrange for them to be taken care of for a few hours, so you are completely free to be present and undistracted by other concerns.

All of this is valuable preparation for you to be in a beautiful, relaxed, and clear state, inwardly and outwardly. You are setting the frequency for your total environment to be most supportive of sacred engagement.

Now you are ready to connect with your partner. I will suggest another activity for you to share. It involves the type of touch and physical connection that opens your body and your heart to your partner.

I recommend a very simple exchange, where the receiving partner describes the kind of touch they like in as much detail as possible and then guides their partner in giving this to them. The giving partner receives the instructions with openness, in the disposition of pure service to their beloved, without trying to superimpose their preferences or suggestions upon their partner's requests or guidance. They simply try to follow what they are being asked to do to the best of their ability. After the receiving partner has requested and received one activity from their partner, they thank their partner and then change roles.

Now the person who was receiving becomes the giving partner and vice versa, for one activity. Keep alternating between receiving and giving, one activity at a time until you are so full, open, and alive with sexual energy that your desire is to transition into lovemaking.

Be sure to stop after receiving one form of giving from your partner and then change roles. The changing from receiver to giver and back again is an important part of the process.

I love you and bless you in your opening to love and God.
I AM Mary Magdalene

Mary's reference at the beginning of her message to me not needing to "make" things happen was in response to a conversation I'd had earlier that morning with a video show host, who was seeing if I was a fit for his show. He not only decided I was perfect but also gave me several leads that might open up some other big opportunities for me.

After receiving this message, I had a productive day, though still feeling stress from having so much to handle, including needing to find a new long-term-care facility for my father.

At 5:00 p.m. I texted Tony: "Want to go for a bike ride?"

He wrote back: "I'd love to. Be over soon." I wrapped up what I was working on, took a shower, and had just finished putting on some makeup when I heard his quiet knock at the front door.

We kissed passionately, threw my bike in his truck, and took off on our adventure. We had a delightful bike ride downtown, finishing as the sun was setting and drinking in a magnificent display of vivid washes of color across the sky, as the sliver of a moon became gradually brighter. We ended the ride with more kisses and delicious, crisp fall apples. On the drive home, we picked up shrimp tacos, which we heartily enjoyed back at my house.

After dinner, we read the transmission I had received from Mary that morning. Tony immediately asked me, "How would you like to be touched?"

Pausing to feel what my body was calling for, I said, "I'd like to have light kisses on the back of my neck." He immediately accommodated my request with exquisite, soft kisses. The touch of his lips sent shivers up and down my back.

Then I asked Tony, "What would you like?"

He told me, "I want very light caresses on my face and neck." He moaned with pleasure as I delicately stroked his cheeks, forehead, eyelids, lips, and neck, surprised that I'd never known before how much he enjoyed being touched in that way.

We moved to the bedroom to continue our exchange. Now it was my turn. I said, "I just want to be held in stillness." Tony held me close, occasionally drawing me to him with strength, which sparked intense energy moving between us.

Then Tony requested, "I'd like light touches and strokes all over my back." I happily responded, moving my hands ever so lightly up and down, across, in circles, and in sensual sweeps over his back.

It was challenging to keep alternating between the roles of receiving and giving. Particularly after giving, it was difficult to drop back into myself and connect with what I wanted. I felt my energy being pulled so strongly into the wave of Tony's pleasure that I was naturally drawn into his experience. I sensed the same was happening for Tony in relation to me. Mary's underscoring the importance of alternating the roles helped us both break out of that energetic pull and create something different, a true weaving together of our rhythms and desires. I realized that Mary was helping us grow into a new capacity of simultaneity, where we're both connected to the movement of our own energy and that of our partner at the same time. This practice was leading us to a greater level of facility and freedom in flowing between our energies, ultimately drawing them together into their own creation.

It was my turn again. "I'd like you to hold and pleasure my

breasts," I said. Tony responded with exquisite rhythms of stillness, movement, and pressure.

Next Tony said, "I want you to ever-so-lightly stroke my pants over my lingam." (*Lingam* is the Tantric term for a man's penis. The literal translation is "wand of light." The corresponding term for a woman's vagina is *yoni*, which means "sacred space.") I ran my hand slowly, with the barest pressure, over his pants, feeling the energy mounting.

Then I said, "I want long, slow, light strokes on my back." The energy was peaking and cresting, as we moved in undulating waves of orgasmic passion.

I was crossing over a transition point, filled with life force from the exercise and deeply desiring Tony inside of me to experience our love and energy in the core of my being. I expressed this to him, and he acknowledged the same feeling arising for him. Then I added, "My yoni is still tender from our lovemaking three nights ago. I feel afraid to make love again."

We held each other close as our longing for each other grew increasingly stronger. I removed the rest of Tony's clothes and took his lingam in my mouth, pleasuring him with great love and feeling.

What happened next is a blur. Somehow my clothes came off. I asked Tony to suck my breast and my arousal became intense. Without intending it, I was opening to his lingam and our bodies were taking over. Tony was going very slowly, allowing me to open and draw him in rather than pressing into me. He seemed to know exactly how much I was ready to receive him and went only that far, waiting for me to open more and take him in further with no pressure or stress.

There was an amazing sense of softness and great love. The practice Mary had given us had already taken us to a depth of love and feeling that was incredible. Now it was carrying us into merging our bodies on a wave of energetic ecstasy that was entirely different from mere physical union. I felt like a dolphin in water, playing in bliss.

Tony was fully inside me now, moving slowly or not at all. The intensity of the energy was astounding and exquisite. We were carried into a depth of sensation that left us in awe. Afterward, we held each other, with so much energy surging through us that Tony began trembling. I suggested that we engage the ankh breathing practice together (see figure 25-1), explaining to Tony how to do it.[1] Holding each other and breathing in this energetic pathway brought even more ecstasy. Tony said he saw a vision of a mandala with incredible colors.[2] We both felt filled with joy, tears flowing from our eyes.

As we kissed again, I had a vision of a huge statue that resembled the Great Sphinx, with its many smaller pyramids. I then noticed that Tony was wearing a necklace that looked Egyptian and asked him, "Where did you get that?"

"I received it as a gift from a man in the Netherlands who's a psychic. He, along with another psychic in Russia, wrote me letters and told me about myself—that I'd had a past life in Mesopotamia as a church elder and powerful healer. They said I was a healer in this lifetime, too. That's the work I'm being called to now. He said I was going to have an incredible love relationship with a woman for the rest of my life, like I'd never known love before. And he told me I was going to be very wealthy because someone in my ancestral line was going to leave me an inheritance."

We were both filled with so much happiness. We couldn't stop kissing each other and holding each other close, in a joyous exchange. Finally around 11:30 p.m. Tony said, "It's time for me to go." After more kisses and embraces he left, ever so sweetly.

The next morning, I received this email from him:

Good morning my love,

What an exquisite experience we had yesterday. It was so beautiful, beginning with our first embrace and kiss. Our bike ride was truly filled with joy—watching the colors of the sky, eating the apples, and the kisses. It was a perfect beginning for what followed.

During the rest of our time together, the energy that passed between us was so powerful, and yet so soft and tender. I give thanks to Mary for all she has shared with you and for your sharing it with me. We have moved into a special place, which is not of this third dimension, a place of complete surrender to each other, with pure bliss as the gift to us.

I slept very well and awoke thinking of you. I spent some time sending you divine healing light for your yoni to not be sore. I trust you will feel better very shortly.

I see your day filled with joy, even with all that you have to accomplish.

I send you soft kisses on your neck, soft touches on your back, and many passionate kisses for your sweet lips. Know that you are loved and I am always with you.

Tony

Figure 15-1. PREPARING FOR SACRED ENGAGEMENT

1. Prepare the physical environment, making it beautiful and honoring of the Goddess.

    a. Make sure the space is clean and pleasing to the senses.

    b. Enhance the beauty of the space through lighting, artwork, sensual music, flowers, and a beautiful and comfortable bed and bedding.

    c. Bring in the sacred through candles, incense, pictures, music, and blessing the space beforehand.

    d. Be sure the temperature is comfortable.

    e. Have water available to drink.

2. Prepare your body so that it's clean and attractive.

    a. Bathe or shower beforehand. Shave, as necessary. Brush your teeth and rinse with mouthwash.

    b. Fix your hair attractively.

    c. Wear attractive clothing that is sensual and comfortable.

3. Allow yourself to be in a relaxed, serene, undistracted state.

    a. Turn off phones and other electronic devices.

    b. Arrange in advance for children (or other responsibilities) to be taken care of for a few hours.

Figure 15-2. EXCHANGING TOUCH

1. Partner A describes the kind of touch they would like in as much detail as possible and then guides Partner B in giving this to them.

2. Partner B receives the instructions with openness, in the disposition of pure service to their beloved, without trying to superimpose their preferences or suggestions. Partner B then follows these instructions to the best of their ability.

3. Partner A thanks Partner B.

4. Change roles, with Partner A becoming the giving partner and Partner B the receiving partner for one activity.

5. Keep alternating between the roles of receiving and giving, for one activity at a time. Continue until you are so full, open, and alive with sexual energy that your desire is to transition into lovemaking.

6. Be sure to stop after receiving one form of giving from your partner and change roles.

SIXTEEN

Kundalini Flow

*T*he next communication came from Mary a day later.

Hello, my dear one,

You are progressing well in integrating the lessons I have been providing. I am well pleased, and I acknowledge your dedication to this work as most valuable and pure. I thank you.

Now we progress to the next step: learning to move the internal energy, or life force. We referred to this energy as the sekhem *in the Egyptian temples. In the Indian tradition it is known as the* kundalini. *Sexuality is an important access way for connecting with this energy.*

Indians portray kundalini as being like a snake or serpent that, in its dormant condition, is coiled up at the base of the spine. When expressed through conventional sexuality, this energy is restricted to the root and sacral chakras and is generally discharged downwardly during orgasm and ejaculation. The same energy is used for creating a new life when conceiving a child. But there is another life-giving function of this energy, which is spiritual transformation and the birthing of your greater, higher-dimensional self. This is the true purpose of sacred sexuality. The exercises I am about to describe are crucial for creating the foundation for this transformational process.

The first skill necessary for engaging sacred sexuality is the ability to connect with energy. For most people, this is a kinesthetic experi-

ence—something they feel. They become able to tangibly sense where the energy is located, how and where it moves, and where it is strong or weak. They have the visceral feeling of something moving within them, like the movement of mercury in an old-fashioned thermometer. They may also have the sensation of being carried by this energy, like riding a wave in the ocean. They may experience the energy as pulsation, throbbing, excitement, or a kind of quickening. (This is how many people experience sexual energy.) It may feel like expansion, engorgement, or heat; like a subtle vibration, a tickling, or electrical energy that's either moving through them or centered in a particular area; or like chills, goose bumps, or chicken skin.

Visually oriented people are often able to see energy as light, colors, or visions. Auditory-based people can hear energy through hearing tone, vibration, or sound. It is even possible to experience energy through certain scents or tastes, though this tends to be more rare. But the primary sensation for most people is kinesthetic.

Other people do not sense energy. These individuals must connect with energy by directing their intention toward it through thoughts or visualization. By doing this they can still engage the process. Oftentimes, they will, over time, open to the ability to sense energy, after practicing and engaging their intention in this manner.

To move your internal energy, begin by first locating it through feeling-awareness. Then consciously relax and breathe into the place in your body where you sense the energy.

Once you are fully connected with your energy, the next step is to maintain this as you connect with your partner's energy. This requires tuning into his or her energy field and using your senses to feel, see, or sense their energy. Then allow yourself to rest in the awareness of both energy fields and their locations.

As you continue to breathe and relax, verbally share with your partner where and how you are experiencing your energy and theirs. Listen as your partner shares where and how they are experiencing their *energy and yours. It does not matter whether your experiences are the same or different. Do not try to change your experiences to match each other's. Simply receive each other's reports.*

Continue breathing and relaxing. Put your awareness on where the energies want to move and follow them. As you do this, verbally share your experience with your partner.

After a period of time, bring this practice to a close, perhaps by taking several breaths together, connecting with your hearts, and then hugging each other. Finally, once again share what you have experienced.

I leave you for now with love and blessings.
I AM Mary Magdalene

After receiving this transmission, I had the thought that Mary was taking me through the steps a priestess would go through while training in the sex magic of Isis. I was curious to experience the effects of this practice.

At lunchtime, Tony and I met for a wonderful meal at India Palace in downtown Santa Fe. While eating, I asked him, "Would you like to join me in learning tango?"

"You know, I've thought about learning tango in the past," he said. "Yes, it would be fun to learn it together." I felt thrilled.

Later I asked Tony something else I'd been thinking about: "I need someone to lead the men's empowerment ritual at my upcoming sacred sexuality workshop. What do you think about doing that?"

He responded thoughtfully. "I'd be interested in doing that. I want to know what you'd like me to do, but we can talk about it." I was delighted, as before. We ended our lunch with plans to get together at 7:30 that evening.

Tony arrived promptly at 7:30. Immediately upon greeting him, I could feel our connection very strongly. As we kissed, I felt my body elongating to reach out to him, creating a tunnel of joy between us.

We read Mary's latest transmission together at my computer and then moved into the bedroom to follow her instruction. We lay down on the bed facing each other and then automatically assumed the position we rest in after making love—Tony on his back with his right arm around me, and me on my left side with my right leg between his legs (see figure 16-1). We naturally fell into a synchronous rhythm of breathing together, our breath slowing down as we deepened in our relaxation.

Figure 16-1. RESTING POSITION

We began by focusing on our own energy. I felt my energy diffused throughout my body, but stronger in my lower abdomen. It was especially activated in my sacral chakra, which felt alive and full of sexual energy.

We then shifted into connecting with each other's energy. At this point I became visual, which was unusual for me, seeing Tony's energy as a golden stream of light from his head to the bottom of his spine and extending down his legs and arms. I was surprised not to see any energy at his genitals. At one point Tony moved his head so that our third eyes were touching, and I saw an intense beam of golden-white light emanating out of this portion of his forehead.

As we began to share our experiences with each other, Tony said, "I saw your energy as a vortex of energy from my sacral chakra up to my third eye chakra. I moved my head to connect to my crown chakra, and after doing that I saw exquisite colors at my crown that are hard to describe. It was something like a yellow light with a kind of violet light around it, but the violet was a color I'd never seen before in this dimension."

"What was your experience of your own energy?" I asked.

"I felt energy from my head all the way down my spine, and going out my arms and legs."

"Did you feel energy in your genitals?" I queried.

"Not really, which seemed strange."

"Wow," I said, "that's exactly how I experienced your energy. How interesting!"

We then continued with the practice. We focused on our combined energies, noticing if they were moving and what we experienced as we followed the energy. The experience again became visual for me. I saw a golden geometric shape forming from our merged energies. It reminded me of a box kite, viewed from an angle, with the endpoints coming out of our third eyes and genitals, and the center connected to our hearts. Then it expanded and shifted into a star tetrahedron around both of us. I sensed that our merkabas had created a field composed of our merged light bodies. It began to spin simultaneously in both directions. Then I saw amazing galaxies, reminding me of Hubble Space Telescope pictures. I felt we were traveling through the cosmos.

At a certain point these galactic visions changed to images of an exquisite crystalline realm, very soft and delicate feeling. I described this to Tony, and he acknowledged experiencing it, too. We naturally sensed a completion point together, and ended by holding, kissing, and hugging each other.

We marveled at the extraordinary beauty we had witnessed. I then asked Tony, "Do you think the reason we both experienced you as not having energy in your genitals was because you might be holding back your sexual energy, sensing it might interfere with your sensitivity to energy in the exercise?"

"I don't think I did that consciously," he replied, "but I think my body was doing it on its own."

"I'd like to try the exercise again," I spontaneously suggested. "This time, consciously allow your sexual energy to be fully present."

As we came together, our bodies immediately began undulating, sometimes powerfully and fast, from the energy moving between us. We kissed and Tony said, "I see sparks between us." The connection became even more powerful as Tony pulled me toward him. Through our clothes, I could feel the tip of his lingam touching my yoni. Our bodies were opening, without us "doing" anything. We both removed our clothes, hungry for more contact.

As often happens for me, I lost some of my feeling of connection through the activity of getting undressed. I asked Tony, "Can we breathe together again, all the way through our genitals?" Almost immediately I felt my connection return. Slowly, I drew Tony inside me and the energy carried us away in a wild current of movement, sound, and powerful sensations. We had an extended orgasm like none we'd experienced before, with our breathing suspended for a long period of time and our bodies moving in perfect synchronicity together. There was no sense of "making" love. We were swept up in a vibrant wave of passion that was moving us in ecstasy.

We came to rest with Tony staying inside me for quite a long time. We felt deeply connected, carried into a fourth-dimensional realm of great spaciousness. I recited a Native American prayer:

"See beauty before me, see beauty behind me, see beauty above me, see beauty below me." Tony spontaneously added, "This is the beauty way."

"Did you know that 'the beauty way' is a traditional Native American expression?" I asked him.

"I didn't know those words. But the Native Americans were able to access the fourth dimension. They understood these kinds of experiences." Tony paused and then said, "Everyone needs to experience this."

Because of my passion for teaching others about sacred sexuality, I felt deep happiness hearing him say that. I very much wanted us to offer this to others together.

We rested more, and I wondered how my yoni was going to feel tomorrow. I had a pattern of going through periods of soreness in the days after our lovemaking. I'd been checked out several times by doctors, and no one could figure out why this was happening. The only thing I could think of was that it had to do with the generous size of Tony's lingam.

"Would you do some healing on my yoni?" I requested. Tony lovingly placed his hand on my yoni and went right to the spot where I was already feeling a burning sensation. I relaxed and deepened into receiving his gentle touch. I opened my legs fully. It felt wonderful to be so open and relaxed, receiving healing energy from Tony after our beautiful lovemaking.

I saw two angels coming down, sending light and healing energy to my yoni. Then I received information in the form of a kind of remembering mixed with new understanding: I realized that my symptoms were related to trauma I had experienced when my daughter was born. As she was ready to come through the birth canal, the doctors determined that I wasn't going to be able to deliver her naturally, as my inner dimensions were too small for the size of her head. They were able to deliver her with a gentle forceps procedure, but in the process I was given an episiotomy and then tore beyond the incision that had been made. Due to the anesthetic I was given, I didn't feel pain at the time, so my only memory of this trauma was at the cellular level.

Becoming aware of the source of my pain felt like a necessary step for the healing to occur. I wondered how much this unconscious pain had affected my relationship with my daughter's father. Was that the beginning of our difficulties? I wondered how much I had closed down without realizing it.

Now I saw a lovely pattern emerging of soft-edged colors with a kind of gentle, lacy design. It felt very feminine and healing, as though I was being returned to the pattern of my wholeness.

Tony slowly moved his hand away and held me. He told me, "I felt an extremely powerful energy come through that was different from anything I'd experienced before. I felt the healing going to your whole abdomen and back, along with your yoni. I also felt a blockage in your upper back that my other hand was moving toward. I want to continue to do healing on you." He hesitated and then added, "What better way to practice healing than to heal you?" I felt so loved.

I was filled with wonder and gratitude for what was happening. How amazing to be receiving this guidance from Mary and to be the "guinea pigs" for trying out these incredible practices.

The next day was the autumn equinox. Tony and I had plans to meet at 7 a.m. with my friend, Audrey, to do a ceremony on the mountain. We parted early so we could both get some sleep. I felt extremely connected to him, sustained in love.

Figure 16-2. EXPERIENCING ENERGY

1. Through feeling-awareness, sense where your energy is located. Consciously relax and breathe into the place in your body where you sense the energy.

2. Maintain your connection to your own energy as you connect to your partner's energy, tuning in to their energy field through the use of your senses or awareness.

3. Rest in the awareness of both energy fields and locations.

4. As you continue to breathe and relax, verbally share with your partner where and how you are experiencing your energy and theirs. Then listen as your partner shares where and how they are experiencing their energy and yours. Do not try to change your experiences to match each other's. Simply receive each other's reports.

5. Continue breathing and relaxing. As you do, put your awareness on where the energies want to move and follow them, sharing your experience with your partner.

6. After a period of time, bring this practice to a close, perhaps by taking several breaths together, connecting with your hearts, and then hugging each other. Finally, once again share what you have experienced.

SEVENTEEN

Tantric Wave

Mary continued her instruction two days after the equinox with this communication.

Hello, dear one,

I am glad you have once again found time to return to meditation and our sessions together. Your work is excellent, and your dedication is most commendable. However, you must remember to stay balanced. Your first work is always to live in God, connected to God, guided by God. Your priority must be to maintain and grow that dedication before your more practical work, including the efforts involved in supporting my communication and that of other light beings who are helping people connect to God. Even this is practical work, and it is still secondary to your primary spiritual work.

Your meditation time is most important. You have noticed how it changes your experience for the entire day. This is because meditation strengthens your connection to your higher-dimensional self, enabling you to increasingly maintain that connection throughout your day. Over time you become able to operate from that higher-dimensional place even if you're not consciously aware of doing so. It is like building up a muscle or a habit.

You have noticed you have resistance to doing this practice daily. You tend to have a rhythm of meditating every second or third day.

This is your current level of comfort for expanding into your higher-dimensional self. If you were to meditate more frequently, your transformation would accelerate, both in terms of its speed and the degree to which you're expanding. You are going at the speed your being is presently ready for, which is fine. When you are ready for more, you will naturally choose that. It is like a built-in control mechanism, a way of applying the brakes, because to go faster would be difficult or scary for you. It is part of your inherent balancing and equilibrium that allows you to progress, change, and grow at the rate that is right for you at any particular time.

Now I would like to go back to our discussion of sacred sexuality. Let's return to the Sea of Galilee. Take my hand, sweet sister, and let us once again walk on the waves. Feel the motion of the water as it carries you. Feel the wind caressing your face, the sun's rays warming your body. Smell the sweet scent of the air. Feel God all around. You are held in love, like a baby in the womb. Yes, I can feel the shift in you. Your body is becoming soft, your heart open. You are in joy and gratitude. And so from this place we begin.

The internal movement of energy, as you know, is the heart of what sacred sexuality is about. We began in the last exercise with strengthening your ability to locate energy—your own and your partner's—and to follow the movement and play of the two energies. You did that very well. As you saw, just that simple exercise is profound and can open up worlds of exploration.

Now you are ready to bring intention to the energy moving up and down the central column of the spine, along the chakras. To begin, you want to connect with the energy at the base of your spine, in the root chakra. Take time to feel, see, and fully connect with the energy there. Breathe into your root chakra. Consciously relax your body and open at the root chakra.

When that is strong, you are going to initiate two steps. They happen simultaneously, but when you are learning them it is easier to do them sequentially. The first step is to begin a movement of arching and rounding your back. It's actually a wavelike motion that starts with arching the pelvis, then the mid-back, then the chest, and finally the shoulders and neck. Keep the arch gentle in the neck, rather than dropping the head too far back, so that the central channel remains open.

Once you are in the full arch position—from your root chakra to your crown chakra—you then reverse the wave by rounding forward, beginning at the top of your central channel. First the head and neck gently come forward, then the chest, mid-back, and finally the pelvis, until you are in a fully rounded shape, like a gentle C. Continue this undulating, wavelike motion of arching up from the base of the spine and then rounding down from the crown of the head.

When you are ready, add the breath to this movement. As you arch up the spine, inhale slowly, filling your whole self with prana, or life force, until the arch crests at the crown chakra. As you round down from the top of the spine, slowly exhale, sending the life force out to your whole self and beyond. Complete the exhalation as the rounding movement reaches the base of the spine.

Continue this pattern of breathing in and arching up the spine, then breathing out and rounding down the spine. Feel the natural rhythm of receiving life energy and then sending it out to your whole self and beyond.

The next step is to see, sense, or feel the energy you connected with at the root chakra moving up the central channel on the inhalation-arching and reaching all the way to the crown chakra. Then see, sense, or feel the same energy moving down the central channel on the exhalation-rounding, going all the way back to the root chakra. This is enough of a practice for a person who is new to this.

Once you are comfortable integrating these three actions—the movement, the breath, and following the energy up and down the spine—you can intensify this practice by raising the sexual energy. It is valuable to do this in the learning phase as a solo practice, stimulating *yourself sexually to raise your sexual energy. A good way to do this is to place your left hand on your heart as you stimulate your genitals with your right hand. Intensifying your experience of energy in this way will help you feel the energy moving up and down your spine more easily.*

Notice the natural rhythm that occurs as the energy moves up to the higher chakras and down to the lower ones. Notice the change in feeling between the upper and lower chakras. Observe your ability to slow down or speed up the energy, or to increase or decrease its intensity. Allow the energy to feed your whole self—all your chakras and spreading out to your whole being.

Be sure to bring your sexual energy all the way down to the root chakra. This is challenging for some people. Rest and open at the root chakra for a moment before beginning the next cycle.

Learn to do this on your own first. With a partner, you can lie side by side in the spoon position, with the woman in front, or you can face each other in various positions.

I love you and shine my light fully upon you.
I AM Mary Magdalene

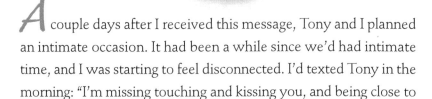

A couple days after I received this message, Tony and I planned an intimate occasion. It had been a while since we'd had intimate time, and I was starting to feel disconnected. I'd texted Tony in the morning: "I'm missing touching and kissing you, and being close to your body."

He replied: "I'm missing that, too. Why don't we get together?"

I suggested: "Let's have intimate time and then eat dinner afterward." I didn't have to twist his arm. I was excited about our plan and felt energized during my work, thinking about our time together later that day. Tony told me later his lingam had immediately responded to our plans.

As he was leaving work, Tony texted me again: "I'll be over a half hour earlier than our original plans." I could tell he was excited about our tryst. I put on a pink satin halter top with black lace trim and black see-through bikini panties, covered over by a pair of slinky black pants and a sparkly midriff top that tied in the front. When I opened the door, Tony looked at me and seemed surprised by what I was wearing. Then he came in and we kissed for a very long time, with great tenderness and passion. We didn't need to talk. Tony asked, "How are you?" three different times, with long spaces of kissing in between.

I said, "I think we should get some ice water to cool us down." We both smiled and moved seamlessly into the kitchen to fill glasses of water, which we carried into my office.

I shared Mary's transmission with Tony, reading it out loud. We went over the technical parts of the practice slowly in our chairs. "As soon as you started reading Mary's instructions," Tony said, "I could feel energy moving up and down my spine."

We moved to the bedroom. I took off my pants and sparkly top, and Tony said, "I really love what you're wearing!" He removed his clothes down to his underwear and we lay down together.

Even though the energy was already strong between us, I said, "I want to start with the sharing practice." We expressed what we were feeling with each other, getting very open and highly aroused as the energy built exponentially. Although we'd intended to try Mary's most recent practice, we instead moved into lovemaking, as that was what we were both feeling strongly called to do.

We moved into the scissors position (see figure 17-1). Tony entered me with perfect sensitivity to my openness, letting me draw him in at my own pace. Our lovemaking was gentle and powerful at the same time, a quality I hadn't experienced before. My heart felt excited and open. During our lovemaking, Tony said, "This is my favorite position because I can be on my side and not put my weight on your body. Plus it gives me a perfect view of our bodies as we're connected." It was all so sweet, while also charged and deeply fulfilling. We made love for a long time.

Figure 17-1. SCISSORS POSITION

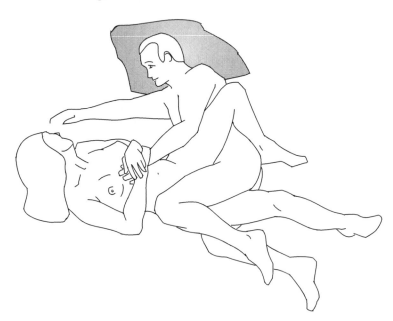

Afterward we held each other, and Tony said softly, "I love this part of our intimacy." I treasured that he was always so present afterward, never falling asleep or getting up to do something else. It felt very much like something Mary had once described as the nesting practice.[1]

I asked Tony, "Would you do some more healing on my yoni?"

"I was just about to offer," he replied. With great tenderness and love, he placed his hand right on the spot where I had soreness, sending me energy. My legs relaxed and opened wide as I drank in his wonderful healing energy. After a while I felt complete, and an instant later Tony gently moved his hand away. I'd noticed much less yoni soreness since the last occasion of his healing. I felt hope that this trajectory of increased well-being would continue.

I received this text from Tony the next day:

Good afternoon, sweetie,

I still feel the glow from our intimacy last night. It was exquisite and also different.

Enjoy your time with your dad today, and enjoy your dancing tonight.

Hugs, kisses, and soft touches,

Tony

Figure 17-2.

1. Connect with the energy in the root chakra at the base of your spine by feeling and seeing the energy there. Breathe into your root chakra. Consciously relax your body and allow yourself to open at the root chakra.

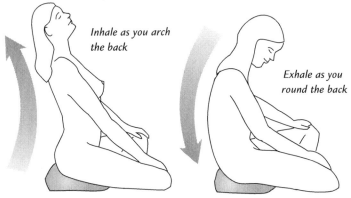

Inhale as you arch the back

Exhale as you round the back

2. Begin a movement of arching and rounding the back. Make it a wavelike motion that starts with arching the pelvis, then the mid-back, then the chest, and finally the shoulders and neck. Keep the arch gentle in the neck so the central channel that runs along the spine remains open.

3. Reverse the wave by rounding down, bringing the head and neck gently forward, then the chest, mid-back, and finally the pelvis, until you are in a fully rounded shape, like a gentle C.

4. Continue this undulating, wavelike motion of arching up from the base of the spine and then rounding down from the crown of the head.

5. When you are ready, add the breath. As you arch up the spine, inhale slowly, filling your whole self with prana, or life force. As you round down from the top of the spine,

TANTRIC WAVE

slowly exhale, sending the life force out to your whole self and beyond.

6. Continue this pattern of breathing in and arching up the spine, then breathing out and rounding down the spine. Feel the natural rhythm of receiving life energy and then sending it out to your whole self and beyond.

7. While continuing this pattern of breathing, see, sense, or feel the energy that you connected with at the root chakra moving up the central channel on the inhalation-arching, reaching all the way up to the crown chakra. Then see, sense, or feel the same energy moving down the central channel on the exhalation-rounding all the way back to the root chakra.

8. When you are comfortable with the integration of movement, breath, and following the energy up and down the spine, intensify the practice by raising your sexual energy. To do this, place your left hand on your heart as you stimulate your genitals with your right hand. Raising your sexual energy in this way will intensify your experience of it, allowing you to more easily feel your energy moving up and down the spine.

9. Be aware of the rhythm of the energy moving up to the higher chakras and down to the lower chakras. Notice the change in feeling between the two. Practice slowing down or speeding up, and increasing or decreasing the intensity. Allow the energy to feed all your chakras and to spread out to your whole being. Be sure to bring the sexual energy all the way down to the root chakra at the end of each cycle, resting and opening there for a moment before beginning the next cycle.

Continued on next page

10. When you feel comfortable with this practice, implement it with a partner, lying side by side in the spoon position, with the woman in front, or facing each other in various positions.

EIGHTEEN

Riding the Crests of the Ocean

Mary's next message came the following morning.

Blessings to you, sweet one,

I am pleased you have chosen to meditate and commune with Spirit this morning, as well as make space for me. I commend and support you in this choice. You can see how much easier it is to engage your meditation practice when you do it more frequently and consistently.

Your intimacy with Tony last night was most beautiful. Both of you were deeply connected and openhearted. Do not be concerned that you did not engage the practice I described in the last transmission. Your choice was appropriate for what you both needed at the time.

This work must not become rigid or rule-like. It is an art, a flow, a dance, a sensitive play—like riding the waves of the ocean. The practices are simply exercises, with guidelines and instruction to help you grow. They give you tools and skills to integrate into your lovemaking. Do not turn them into boxes or cages of confinement. Just as a musician practices scales and arpeggios yet does not play them in concert, so it is for you.

Nonetheless, these practices are important. While you are learning them, adhere to the form. Once you master them they will become a part of you. Then you can bring them into your intimacy in a creative and organic way.

For example, the exercise of moving the sexual energy up and down the spine can be engaged as a solo practice or in partnership. It can be done purely energetically or in combination with being physically engaged. When incorporated into your occasions of intimacy, you may choose to do it during your initial connection with your partner, as a type of foreplay for building sexual energy; in the midst of intercourse, possibly in combination with other forms of lovemaking; or after orgasm. It is for you to experiment with and select what best serves you, your partner, and your intimacy.

Regardless of how you choose to implement this practice, remember to bring the energy all the way down to the root chakra and open fully there. This is essential for this practice to be effective.

I love you and bless you and am with you always.

In love,
I AM Mary Magdalene

I'd woken up that morning feeling rested, happy, and very calm. Having considered Mary's previous communication, I was aware that I had a choice to speed up or slow down my transformation by increasing or decreasing the frequency of my meditation practice. I sensed Mary's compassion and nonjudgment regarding this choice, and thus felt released from my self-judgment. In this state of freedom, I could feel my desire for growth. So while my prior rhythm of meditating every other day would have meant waiting until the following morning to meditate, I had instead chosen to meditate this morning. The process was easier and faster, going through the structured part of my meditation in about five minutes, as opposed to the usual fifteen or so minutes.

Over the next three days, I continued with the daily meditation practice, even as I participated in a dance convention in Albuquerque. After my final dance class, I met my stepmother to look at other assisted-living homes for my dad to move into. He was now spending his days in a wheelchair, so we were interested in a facility that could support his newfound mobility.

The following day was October 1 and the beginning of a new workweek for me. I sat at my computer trying to get something done but didn't have the juice for it. I distracted myself by reading various emails and Web posts, soon landing on an article by Lion Goodman titled "Dorothy and the Very Bad Awful Disowned Feelings," which discussed how physical illness is caused by beliefs. I immediately thought about my yoni soreness. My rational mind said it was because of Tony's generous size and our prolonged and vigorous lovemaking. But I began to wonder if it actually was a result of my beliefs. I read on.

Goodman recommended answering a series of questions to change your current situation. I got into it and worked on answering the questions for the rest of the day, going back over each one several times, more deeply with every pass. By the end of the evening, I was starting to have some breakthroughs:

What experience or feeling am I successfully avoiding by having this condition persist?

I'm avoiding opening more deeply to love and getting hurt by finding out that I care more about Tony than he cares about me. I'm also avoiding losing myself through sexuality, which might lead me to really opening to Tony and, as a result, losing my independence, or autonomy.

What is the payoff I get from having this exact condition?

My yoni soreness requires me to be authentic with Tony and more assertive about my sexual needs, desires, and preferences. It also supports me in having sex that's more energy based rather than primarily physical.

At a deeper level, my yoni soreness puts me in touch with my inner child, who seems to be calling out for love and attention that's not based in sex. This leads me to explore other aspects of our relating. Is Tony available to spend the kind of time with me that I want apart from sex? Will he help take care of me when I need help? Is he taking responsibility for this situation with me?

What beliefs do I have that could create a condition like this?

Men only love and value me for sex. To be loved, I have to be beautiful, sensual, and willing to give men what they desire sexually.

If I show who I really am and reveal my needs (including my inner child needs and that I want my partner to practice Tantric sex with me), I won't be loved.

What beliefs would create the scenario I would rather have?

My value and worthiness to be loved come from who I am, not what I do or how I appear. All the parts of myself are worthy of love and being valued.

Showing who I really am and what my needs are helps others see my divine nature and love me for that.

I can take care of my own needs, including my inner child needs and my desire for Tantric sex, and attract a partner who will also care about my needs.

I can have a Tantric sexual relationship that's fulfilling to me and my partner.

Am I willing to change my beliefs?

Yes!

I started to comprehend that my yoni soreness was really my body telling me that I didn't want to be in relationship with Tony.

This revelation brought a sense of peace, which surprised me. At the same time, I was aware that other discoveries might surface as I continued to delve into my beliefs.

NINETEEN

Synchronicity

The next morning as I lay in bed, I questioned the conclusion I'd come to the night before. While the unconscious beliefs I'd uncovered seemed genuine, and the importance of releasing them both necessary and liberating, that didn't automatically mean that I should dump Tony. In the clear light of a new day, I recognized that letting go of Tony was just another strategy for assuming separation to protect myself from getting hurt. I cautioned myself about my tendency to quickly bail out of relationships, reaffirming a commitment I'd made some time ago to curb my knee-jerk reaction to discard a partner whenever I suddenly decide he isn't right for me.

In the evening, I went to the dance studio for my usual Tuesday night class. Afterward, Tony arrived for his first tango lesson. It was so wonderful to see him, partly because our two days apart was feeing like forever, but even more so because seeing him at the dance studio seemed to draw my two worlds together. I went over to him, beaming, and said, "Hello," as I rubbed his back.

He looked happy to see me, too, but also a little reserved. After a few moments of connecting, we shared a slightly shy kiss. Then he asked, "Would you like to spend time together later?"

"I'll go food shopping now," I replied, "and come back after your class."

Tony met me outside just as I was returning. He told me about his lesson, and we danced tango together on the sidewalk in the strip mall, which felt delightful and very romantic. Then we drove to my house.

We unpacked the groceries and ate fruit together, finishing by sharing a scrumptious—perfectly ripe, soft, and very sweet—fig. Then Tony said, "I have a surprise for you." He handed me a star tetrahedron that had been carved from jasper, which he'd mounted on a handsome cherry wood base. This was very special to me because I connect with the star tetrahedron shape of my merkaba daily as part of my meditation practice. I was very moved that he'd made this for me and delighted in the star tetrahedron standing perfectly upright. I felt very loved.

We placed the carved piece on my office altar. Then Tony said, "You mentioned working with questions and answers yesterday. Would you like to share that with me?"

I felt very vulnerable sharing it with him, worried that he'd feel criticized or pushed away. But honoring my commitment to practice transparency in our relationship, I dove in. After reading the first question and my responses, Tony replied, "I have the same fear—that I care more about you than you do about me." We were both amazed to discover that we shared the same feeling about each other. Then Tony added, "I actually have the other fears you mentioned, too—of getting hurt, losing control, and losing my independence, or autonomy." We felt even more struck by our similarity.

I continued sharing my questions and answers with Tony, who really seemed to "get" my beliefs, especially when I told him about my childhood syndrome of having repeating headaches (which was a way of asking for love and closeness from my mother through a physical ailment) and my father's distant relationship with me (leading me to doubt my worthiness of love and caring from men).

I ended by expressing my fear that men would only want me for sex, or wouldn't want to have Tantric sex with me.

After I finished I felt even more vulnerable. I wondered what Tony thought about all that I'd shared. He told me, "I think we should stop having sex for now."

I loved having sex with Tony and feared that without it we would grow distant. Besides, not having sex would not resolve the core issues, such as caring for my inner child needs. I replied, "I'd like to hold refraining from sex as one possible course of action while we explore other options as well."

Tony seemed perplexed. "What else could we do?"

"One thing is that we could talk more about some of the questions I raised," I said. "For example, I don't know very much about your intentions and plans for the future."

That request seemed to open the floodgates to Tony's inner world. He began speaking very openly about himself and his concerns. He explained that he'd been helping his ex-wife get the medical care she needs and how frustrating it was to work with the healthcare system. He talked for quite a while, and I sensed it was helping him release a great deal of pent-up energy he'd been holding in. When he finished, I was feeling turned on and wanting to connect physically. When I told him that, he said, "Yes, I noticed I'm feeling turned on, too! It's remarkable how talking about the real stuff that's going on opens our energy and connects us."

Tony paused as he tapped into something deeper. "This is really different to be talking about such profound things together. I haven't done that before with a partner. I may have touched on things with select people, but I've never revealed what was going on to the depth that we do.

"Do you remember when I told you how much I loved the scissors position because my weight wasn't on top of you and I could see your whole body? That was really new for me to make a comment like that. It was incredible to be in that position and realize how much I loved it. I had to remind myself that this wasn't a movie I was watching—it was my life!"

Tony continued, "I don't just want you for sex. I love your for all of who you are. What I value the most is the way I feel when I'm with you. The last time that we were apart, I felt like something big was gone from my life. I'm so glad I texted you and told you. I was thinking you'd probably moved on, especially when I didn't hear back from you right away. When you said you were missing me, too, I was so relieved."

I started thinking about the soreness I'd been experiencing. "You know," I said, "the soreness doesn't appear immediately after our sexual occasions but rather one or two days later. That makes me think it's not about abrasion. After all, if you skin your knee, it doesn't start hurting one or two days later. Maybe I should start noticing what's going on for me when the soreness flares up. This might give me clues about what's triggering it. In fact, yesterday as I was thinking about what I might be avoiding through the yoni soreness or what the payoffs of my experience were, my yoni soreness suddenly flared up—and we hadn't had sex in five days!" I felt a great sense of promise upon suddenly realizing that the actual cause of my pain could be thoughts I was having, not our sexual activity.

Emboldened by everything I was hearing, I decided to take a leap of faith and share something I'd been holding back on. "I've been feeling scared to bring this up, but I want to talk about it in the spirit of sharing everything in intimacy. It's about something that happened during the equinox ritual we did with Audrey. I was very moved by the way the three of us flowed together so seamlessly and naturally, with you and I drumming together the entire hike in and out in perfect timing, our drums in perfect tune with each other's, and Audrey leading the way, shaking a rattle. Without talking, we moved directly into a spontaneous celebration at the precise moment of the equinox, offering singing, poetry, prayers, and flute playing. Then we manifested a delicious feast and a blessing of the water. It was all so smooth and effortless.

"In the midst of doing all that, I started to think that maybe Audrey should join our relationship. We could become a threesome. I even saw us all living together. I immediately censored myself, thinking I'd probably completely mess up my relationship with you if I even mentioned it, let alone try to do anything about it. So I decided not to say anything to you about it."

To my amazement, Tony replied, "I had the very same thought and immediately cut it off. I figured you'd be upset, thinking I was more attracted to Audrey than to you."

Some part of me wasn't surprised to hear this. I must have suspected that the same thought had crossed Tony's mind. *Maybe we were all lovers together in a past life,* I told myself.

I noticed I was feeling kind of weird and Tony said he was, too. We left it there, having a sense of completeness for now, which felt good.

Our conversation shifted to talking about our inner children. As we became more lighthearted and playful, I said, "I think your inner child wants to come out and play."

"I've actually been thinking about that the past few days," Tony agreed. "My inner child needs nurturing." *Another synchronicity!* I thought.

"Maybe we should hook up our inner children and set them up on a date," I bantered. We started talking about dressing up for Halloween, describing costumes we'd had as kids and costumes we'd made for our own kids. By now we were lying next to each other on the loveseat, cuddling and kissing intermittently between bouts of laughter.

Finally I said, "I'm getting tired," and Tony checked his watch. It was 1:15. Fllled with joy, we got up, embraced, and kissed. Then Tony left. As I watched him head out the door I marveled at the sweetness of our time together.

I went to bed after 3:00 a.m., with my heart open and vibrant sexual energy coursing through me. I had a powerful self-pleasuring session, bringing myself to a deep and full orgasm with waves of ecstasy washing over me.

TWENTY

Timeless Connection

*E*arly the next day, Tony sent a text:

Good morning, sweetie,

Slept really well and woke up to a golden river of light swirling within my third eye. It was truly beautiful and so soothing. Then it shifted to a gray and black pattern, which was also quite amazing and actively moving. I watched with my eyes closed and then realized that I was moving through space at a high speed. I recognized where I was from an artist's conception of the outer space regions, a part of creation that is known in the higher realms that's outside the seven super-universes. I was experiencing the beginning of this part of creation. The individual space bodies were more than three hundred million light years across, and I was passing them as if they were grains of sand. I felt my oneness with all of creation.

I will stop here, as the rest is beyond words. But I will say that all is in divine order. I felt the need to share this with you, even if you don't understand.

Adonai,

Tony

This was followed by a second text:

I was thinking about our talk last night. I feel these verbal exchanges are very powerful and heart opening, and definitely make a huge difference in our feelings for each other. It's as if a switch gets turned on and I want to be intimate right then. It's really obvious when that shift happens.

This is quite a process, and I feel the transparency is a big part of it. It has removed so many barriers and allowed us to relate without fear of being vulnerable. I see joy and peace being a big part of our lives as we remove the factors that limit us.

Have a beautiful and productive day.

Much love to you,

Tony

Right away, I received a third text from Tony:

I really want you to know that I want you for all of who you are, not just to have sex with you. That's important. Remembering how I felt when we were apart for just a week said a lot about our relationship and its value in my life. Sex is a part of the whole picture, but it's only one of the many things we share. The different aspects are like spokes of a wheel. They all play a role in keeping the wheel moving.

I'm happy we're working on all aspects. I'm happy you can share everything with me.

My heart is open, and I want you soon. I'm not sure I can wait until Friday like we'd planned. Can I come by around 1:30 today?

I condensed my work into the next couple of hours, eager to get ready for an afternoon rendezvous with Tony. I put on a blue satin teddy he hadn't seen before, covering it with a soft blue caftan. The doorbell rang at exactly 1:30. Without a word, we melted into a passionate kiss, with Tony's hand stroking down my back. I wondered if he could feel the teddy beneath my dress.

Tony had brought over tamales. We ate and talked about our day. He told me, "Many people are starting to feel a sense of disturbance, which I think is going to increase as we move closer to the center of the galaxy on December 21." He also talked about the amazing vision he'd had that morning and how his understanding of it correlated with his studies of the Urantia teaching.[1]

"Do you think the vision was related to the process we went through last night?" I asked.

"Definitely," he affirmed.

We went into my office to reread Mary's instruction about moving sexual energy up and down the spine, reading it section by section and refreshing ourselves on the various parts. We still hadn't followed this instruction yet because the last time we'd made love we got swept away with passion. This time our resolve was stronger.

I put on some sensual, slow music as Tony got ice water for us to drink, knowing how hot we tended to get while making love. Setting the drinks down, Tony removed all his clothes down to his underwear. I followed suit, slipping off my caftan. Tony was surprised and excited when he saw me in the teddy. "Wow, you look fantastic!" he exclaimed with obvious delight. We immediately started kissing and caressing. Our passion was high. I could feel myself wanting to just let go and flow with the strong current of arousal that was carrying us both. But I remembered my resolve to choose to practice Mary's instruction, as well as to have Tantrically based sex, rather than just going with my instinctual drive.

I asked Tony, "Do you still want to do the practice?"

"What practice?" he responded, and we both laughed.

Then I turned so we were in the spoon position, with my back resting against Tony's chest, our knees bent and touching. We started moving together as Mary had described, undulating in waves up and down our spine. Without a word, we added conscious breathing and visualizing sexual energy moving up to the crown and back down to the root chakra. We continued for quite a while, moving into a deep trance state that was pleasurable, calm, and deeply connected.

Again without talking, we sensed we were ready to transition to something else. Facing each other once more, we returned to kissing and caressing. Now the energy was noticeably different. Our raw passion had been elevated to something quite sublime and exquisitely sensitive. Tony ever so slowly slipped the spaghetti straps of the teddy down over my shoulders, arms, and hands, and then slowly removed it. I mirrored his movement, taking down his shorts in slow motion as he relaxed on his back. I stroked deliberately up from his feet, along the inside of his legs to his lingam, cupping his lingam with my hands. It seemed like a sacred object of Masculinity and God-force, and I was a grateful worshipper. I moistened my hands with my saliva and began pleasuring his wondrous instrument of divine love adoringly with my hands and mouth. Tony groaned and sighed with delight.

I stretched my body up beside him, our mouths kissing and energy openly flowing between us. Tony whispered, "I want to give you pleasure, too."

"I'm receiving so much pleasure from what we're doing," I reassured him. "I don't feel moved to do anything different." I continued honoring Tony's lingam, spreading lubricating gel over him to more expressions of delight from him. Then I mounted him and we moved into exquisite lovemaking.

I don't remember what happened after that, other than a few fleeting memories of amazing orgasms and powerful rhythms of total synchronicity between us. I know we made love for a long, long time, and I remember being transported to realms of bliss. At one point I looked into Tony's eyes and was amazed at what I saw. "I feel like I'm gazing into the eye of a whale," I murmured.

Finally I said to him, "I want to rest now, and I want you to stay inside of me." We then began our deep breathing and undulating again, moving the energy up and down our spines. But this time it was intensely magnified, especially as we moved the energy to the root chakra. We would move the energy up and down a few times and then experience another full-body orgasm, continuing this again and again.

Suddenly a new pathway of energy opened up, causing us to feel as though we had a shared column of energy between us. During each orgasmic release, the energy rushed up this shared central channel like fireworks shooting upward into the night. Then Tony would smile and say, "Again," and we would start the pattern once more. We did this for quite a few cycles until we once again came to rest.

I sensed we'd gone through a significant transition—Tony had experienced the full power of moving sexual energy through his central column in the midst of lovemaking. All the previous practices had been leading to this, and the pieces of the bigger picture were coming together. I felt he wasn't just doing this for me anymore. Now he was following his own ecstasy and movement of energy. Once more, he repeated what he'd declared so many times before: "Everyone needs to experience this!"

During our closing cycles of moving our sexual energy up and down our spines, I had a powerful insight: I saw our bodies as having two poles—one at the crown of the head and one at the base of the spine. I perceived the crown as the Masculine pole and the root chakra as the Feminine pole. As we moved the sexual energy up and down the spine, I felt us sharing each of those energies with its opposite. The sexual energy cresting at the top was the Feminine in her peak of life force, reaching out to meet her lover, the Masculine, at the crown pole. As the energy descended the spine in combination with the exhaled breath, it came to rest at the bottom in archetypal emptiness, the quintessential Divine Masculine state of pure consciousness, embracing his lover at the Feminine pole. The new pathway created between us through our shared orgasm was the Divine Child, bursting forth with blessings of love and consciousness into the world.

We came to rest in our usual position. "I really love this part of our sex," Tony softly affirmed, as we basked in the slow, deep pleasure of holding each other, fully drinking in our connected stillness after our more intense loving.

Moments later, Tony asked, "What made this occasion so different?"

"It was the practice we implemented. We moved into the etheric realm and were making love from there while still immersed in the physical realm." We looked at the clock and it was 6:00 a.m. We were incredulous that so much time had passed in what seemed like a brief, delicious space of timeless connection.

TWENTY-ONE

Clearing Attachments

I slept deeply and woke up feeling energized, filled with love, and clear. My yoni felt fine, which I was grateful for since I wanted to be in good condition for the day. I had a life-coaching session with a client in the morning, a radio interview in the afternoon, and a dance class in the evening. Additionally, I was hoping to draft a newsletter.

I meditated and then noticed the initial signs of soreness—a feeling of queasiness and disturbance in my yoni and sacral chakra. Taking a yellow citrine crystal that I keep next to a statue of Isis on my altar, I placed it over my sacral chakra. Then I positioned a quartz Goddess crystal that I keep by my altar picture of Mary Magdalene at the base of my yoni. The crystal at my yoni felt very strong and immediately removed all feelings of discomfort. In contrast, I felt numb at my sacral chakra and couldn't connect with the crystal there at all.

I asked myself, *What beliefs am I holding in my yoni and sacral chakra?* The answer came immediately: *I'm bad.* It was connected to feeling shame. I then asked, *What payoff am I getting from having the yoni soreness?* The answer I received was, *Punishment and cleansing.*

141

The answers felt true to me, yet I was in disbelief that these could actually be my beliefs. Then I flashed on a healing I'd had in 1997, which involved a past lifetime in ancient Egypt. I was an adolescent girl who'd been captured by a very dark cult of men. They convinced me I was bad and impure, and proceeded to "purify" me through sexual torture, rape, and eventually murder. Remembering my brutal lifetime in Egypt, I suddenly registered that I could still be harboring those beliefs subconsciously.

I started to feel there were two beings inside me—one who held my conscious beliefs and another who believed I was bad and impure. I determined that the second one wasn't me but rather an entity I'd taken on and housed at some point. I had attracted it to myself by becoming convinced I was bad, and I would continue to house and feed it as long as this belief persisted.

I told the entity, "I want you to leave. Are you willing to go and leave me alone?" It responded in the affirmative. I began to release the entity, as I'd been trained to do. I could feel the entire clearing as it occurred. After the being left, my body felt extremely quiet and calm. I also felt a vulnerability in my sacral, solar plexus, and throat chakras that was clearly different from before. I spent time sending healing to those chakras and then applied essential oils to them.

Afterward I still felt vulnerable. I wished I didn't have so much to do and could simply curl up in bed and nurture myself. My sacral chakra seemed much more open than normal. I sent it beams of love carrying the message "You are a perfect divine manifestation." It felt good, new, and shaky, all at the same time.

Midmorning, I received a text from Tony:

Good morning, sweetie. Hope you slept well. Had you on my mind this morning, so I thought I would write and let you know.

Still thinking of our afternoon together. Just wanted to thank you again, and to thank Mary for the process. It all happened with such grace, almost as if we were in a dream state. It was exquisite.

Have a beautiful day, filled with joy and tranquility.

Your joyful lover,

Tony

Soon after, my stepmother called to say my dad was going to be relocating to a second rehabilitation facility in order to receive more physical therapy. Now he'd have more time to work with a physical therapist named Eddie, the only one who had gotten my dad to transfer in and out of his wheelchair on his own. Unlike the other therapists who tried to coach my dad when he didn't want to do something, Eddie would just say, "OK, let me know when you're ready," and give him space.

The other therapists had reported that my dad was resistant and no longer making progress. Yet it seemed to me that they were also resisting what he wanted. The law of attraction appeared to be creating a mirror on both sides of this difficulty. When Eddie offered no opposition, my dad would find his own way to cooperate.

As the day continued, I experienced a mild amount of yoni soreness, but not nearly as much as I'd experienced at other times. I felt strong emotionally and didn't collapse or get afraid when I started to feel the distress in the way I typically did. I thought it was natural that I should have some soreness because I was still healing at the physical level. But I wasn't at the mercy of this pattern because my core belief had changed. I sent love and light to my yoni, confident that it was healing.

TWENTY-TWO

Trust

That evening, Tony was going to meet me at a dance studio practice party, but he never showed up. While getting into my car to drive home, I saw I had a text from him that read: "I'm not going to make it tonight. I'm tired from work and don't feel up to coming. I hope to see you tomorrow night."

I was disturbed. *Why doesn't he prioritize seeing me over the work he's doing?* I wondered. *And tomorrow night he will be recording with the choir, so we won't be together.* I didn't respond to his text, partly out of resentment and partly because I wanted to calm down before communicating with him.

Tony called the next morning as I was getting ready to leave for Albuquerque to help my dad move to the new facility. "Can I call you back when I'm driving?" I asked. I thought he heard the shortness in my voice.

I ended up leaving for Albuquerque later than I wanted and felt stressed by the time we talked. "Relax and breathe," Tony gently reminded me. I appreciated the sweetness of his "fatherly" concern and realized I needed some Masculine force to redirect my energy. "I'm visualizing you having plenty of time for everything you want to do," he added. I felt doubtful but hoped he was right.

I knew I needed to express my upset about the night before. "I felt dejected and hurt that you didn't come to the dance party," I told him.

"I understand," he replied, "but I wasn't up to coming. I would like to see you tonight if you're up for that."

"You're recording with the choir tonight," I reminded him.

"Oh yeah, I forgot about that." He seemed frustrated. "Well, we could get together afterward."

"No," I said, "that will be too late."

Tony then suggested, "How about if I call you when we're done, and I'll see how you're doing?"

"OK." I felt tense and not very connected to him.

It turned out I had plenty of time to do everything I wanted with my dad, just like Tony had suggested. In fact, the timing was perfect. I got to talk to two of my dad's therapists and a patient I'd befriended, all of whom I wanted to see before my dad checked out. I packed up all his stuff while he brushed his teeth and shaved, which I hadn't seen him do for himself in over six months. We had a lovely "last lunch," and just as we finished his transport arrived to take him to the new rehab center.

I liked the new facility very much. It felt professional yet warm, and I was impressed with the staff I met. The stress of the move had made my dad nervous, but I kept joking with him and could tell he was reassured by my presence. In fact, no sooner did I get him moved than he fell asleep so deeply that I couldn't wake him to say good-bye.

Before returning to Santa Fe, I decided to hit the mall and check out the Columbus Day sales. I picked up some makeup and then headed to Victoria's Secret. I had so much fun trying on different outfits, dancing in the dressing room to the sensual music coming through the speakers, while the attentive sales associates scurried about, finding more lingerie for me to test out. I ended up selecting a sexy bra and panty set. By then my energy was soaring.

As I headed for my car, I texted Tony: "I've been shopping and you're going to *love* what I got!"

He could tell my energy had changed. He texted me back: "I'd love to see what you got."

Soon a second text arrived: "I really want to see you. Are you free tomorrow afternoon at 2:00? We could go to Chow's later for dinner?"

I called him, since I was driving and couldn't text. "I'd love to get together tomorrow," I said and meant it. We agreed he'd call that night after his recording session.

During my drive home, I reflected on my tendency to assume the worst. I'd done it with my dad that morning and with Tony the night before. Yet even though I was disappointed that Tony hadn't come to the practice party, I still had a really good time dancing with everyone else. In that moment, I recognized something new about myself: although I tended to assume everything wasn't OK when they didn't go as I'd planned, I could assume the "OK-ness" of the bigger picture. This meant I could still maintain trust in God and life when things didn't seem to be going my way—and I could do so without suppressing my feelings. It was about staying connected to my Masculine side of transcendence.

Tony did call after the choir gathering and, to my surprise, I felt like seeing him. When he arrived, he asked, "Would you like to share what you've been through?" I was touched that he brought it up and wanted to know. I told him about the healing I'd gone through with my yoni and the breakthrough I'd had around trusting that things are OK. He was excited by my news. We talked and hugged and kissed, celebrating my steps forward.

Then we booked a ticket for Tony to join me in Austin, Texas, at the end of the month, when I was planning to take a trip there with my daughter, Celeste, to visit my mom and stepdad. Celeste and I were going to drive out together. Then she would fly home from Austin, and Tony would be with me for the drive back. I felt very loved.

TWENTY-THREE

Sexy Lingerie

The next morning I hit the ground running, trying to catch up on work. I was busy till early afternoon, when I stopped to get ready for my date with Tony. I put on the bra and panties I'd gotten the day before, and then picked out a pretty velvet top Tony had never seen and a pair of velour pants, thinking about his enjoyment of soft material. Finally I put on the new makeup I'd also gotten on my shopping spree and felt pretty.

I thought about picking out some music, but somehow my energy wasn't there. In fact, I wasn't really up for having a romantic occasion at all. I felt kind of off. I hadn't meditated that morning, and I felt disconnected from my heart. But mostly I was disappointed to no longer be feeling amorous like the day before.

Tony arrived, and my energy started to perk up. He was clearly happy to be together, and I felt his love and energy. I told him I hadn't meditated and felt kind of strange, and he immediately suggested, "Why don't we meditate together?"

I loved the idea! It felt like a very intimate thing to do together. Meditating with my partner was something I'd often longed for and I'd wondered what it would be like to make love after meditating together.

"Recently I've been thinking that I'd like to teach you the meditation I do," I told him, "because I think it's the perfect complement to Tantric lovemaking. It's a kind of inner lovemaking between your heart and your brain."

"Yes, I'd be open to learning that," Tony responded. Again, I so appreciated his energy and enthusiasm for what I wanted!

"I think it would take two sessions," I explained. Tony was fine with that, too. We decided to do the first session right away.

My explanation took about forty-five minutes, during which Tony had great attention for the process. Afterward he said, "I feel like there's a lot more energy around my head and a lot of expansion I haven't felt before. It's similar to having an energetic helmet around my head, like a half a sphere over the top of my skull."

Then we sat and meditated at my altar. It felt wonderful to do that together. For me, it was very emotional to share something that's so special with my beloved. Tony said he could really feel our connection while we were meditating.

After meditating, we continued moving very slowly. Everything was incredibly sensual and pleasurably charged. I asked Tony, "Are you ready to see what I bought?"

He gave me an enthusiastic "Yes!" I smoothly took off my top and pants, revealing my new lingerie. Tony was really wowed, exclaiming, "You make me feel special when you wear such exquisite lingerie. I love your body, and I think you're very beautiful." I loved his response to me and my outfit.

After a long time of enjoying my sexy underwear, we slowly transitioned into making love. I felt soft and open, and we made love very passionately for a long time. At one point, Tony commented, "You seem different with the entity gone, like you're the only one here now. You feel really good."

Before we knew it, 6:00 p.m. had arrived. We got dressed and went out for a fantastic Chinese meal, followed by a movie. It was a lovely cap to our day.

TWENTY-FOUR

Dreams

I slept in the following morning, waking up gradually. When I got to my desk, I saw this text from Tony:

> Good morning, sweetie. You've been on my mind since I awakened. I'm still feeling myself being inside of you. I'm missing you—the precious time we shared yesterday afternoon and our wonderful dinner after. Also the sexy bra and soft panties . . . mmmmmmmmmmm. Hope you slept well and are enjoying this cool Sunday morning. I love you and look forward to seeing you soon.
>
> Your joyful lover,
>
> Antonio

I was still feeling him inside of me, too. I texted him back, telling about an inspiration I'd had for a gathering I'd like to lead. I asked if he wanted to come over and hear about it. The next thing I knew, the phone was ringing and it was Tony. "Hi, sweetie. I can't come over because I'm getting ready for another recording session with the choir. But I could come over afterward, around three."

"That sounds great. I could make a late lunch for both of us," I offered.

"Good. I'll call you when we finish."

I began working on my new idea, which involved adapting the chakra resonance practice into an individual process that could be led as a guided meditation in group occasions. Later I took a break to pick up salmon for our lunch and some golden beets (one of Tony's favorites). I already had a couple of great artichokes to complete the meal. Then I went back to work and awaited his call before fixing the meal.

The next time I looked at the clock, it was 4:15 p.m. Wondering if the recording session was still going, I texted Tony and he wrote back: "I stopped by to see Lucas. I was just getting ready to leave and come over." Lucas was his grandson who lived in town.

I immediately got upset, my stomach churning and thoughts boiling. *Why doesn't he call and let me know he's changed his plans?* I asked myself. *What about asking me if that's OK with me?* I'd been waiting to see him and to eat. *Don't I matter?*

I texted him: "I get upset when we have plans and then you do something else without letting me know or asking if that's OK. I need to matter."

He texted back: "I'm sorry. Do you still want me to come over?"

I felt torn. I was upset, and worried that I'd say something I'd regret. At the same time, I trusted that if we got through this it would bring us closer. We had an amazing track record of never having a fight, even though we'd gone through some difficult situations before. So I wrote: "Yes, I want you to come over and work through it with me." He showed up three minutes later.

Even when I'd been upset with Tony in the past, I'd never felt like he was my enemy and I would quickly remember that I loved him. Maybe it was because he was so undefended or because I was finally getting more balanced emotionally. In any case, when he arrived I took him by the hand and we went back to my bedroom. After settling on the bed, I asked him, "So what happened?"

"You're right," he began. "I made a choice to do something other than what we'd agreed. I thought it would be quick, but it turned out to be longer than I anticipated. I'm sorry."

"I appreciate your apology, but I need to be able to count on you doing what you say. And I need to matter."

"I want you to be able to count on me. And you do matter. It's just been a long time since I've seen Lucas and I've been missing him. Would it have made a difference if I'd called?" he asked.

"Definitely," I responded. "I was looking forward to seeing you, and I was waiting to eat together. Naturally I felt disturbed when you didn't show up, and hurt when I found out you'd decided to do something else without even telling me. If you'd called, we could have talked about what you were thinking of doing. When we have plans to be together and you want to make a change, I want to be asked if it's OK with me."

"I can understand that," he said.

"I want you to see Lucas," I explained, "and I probably would have supported you in spending time with him. But I want to be included in the decision if it involves changing what we've planned. That's part of cocreating our lives."

"I agree," Tony affirmed. "I want to do what you're describing. This won't happen again."

By the end of our talk, I felt resolved and at peace. I was relieved to have cleared my disturbance so easily and to be open to him again. I beamed with happiness like the sun coming out after a storm. My body had relaxed and I felt drawn to Tony. We started snuggling and kissing, enjoying being close. Then I remembered a funny YouTube video I'd seen and wanted to share with him.

We watched *Shit New Age Girls Say to Boys*, followed by *Shit Boys Say in Response to New Age Girls*, laughing and joking. I was wearing a jean skirt with kneesocks, and we kidded that I looked like a schoolgirl. I explained, "I chose this outfit so my yoni could breathe. I'm not wearing any underwear because I want my yoni to be in fresh air." I had some mild soreness, but nothing like I'd had in the past, which I was really celebrating.

"I like the idea of your not wearing panties," Tony responded. "That's very sexy!"

By now we were both hungry. We went into the kitchen and made dinner together. While we were eating, Tony mentioned a five-acre property he was thinking of buying for his son and daughter-in-law. I instantly felt jealous and shot back, "What about us?" I had a dream of the two of us getting a house together and I was picturing it being relegated to the back burner indefinitely, while he focused on creating a home for his kids and grandson.

"Actually, there's a twenty-five-acre property I've been considering for us," he confided. "I think it might be a good place for building a home, retreat center, and community, including having some families live there as caretakers."

I was blown away. He continued to describe his vision of us living in a rural area about ten miles outside of town. It included everything I'd fantasized about in my ideal life. The more he talked, the more loved I felt. I must have said five times, "This is incredible!" And I meant it.

We parted full of love and joy, with plans to see each other the following evening.

PART II

Intermediate Practices

TWENTY-FIVE

Orbs

I was happily surprised to hear from Mary the next morning.

Beloved sister of my heart,

Hello, dear one. It has been a while since we have talked, and I am happy to reconnect with you. You are in a very good space of heart, mind, and body with regard to all we are working on together. I am well pleased and commend you for your diligent work and devotion to what we are bringing forth. I say we because this is manifesting through both my instruction in my messages and your knowledge base, along with your application of the material and willingness to share your story of it. This wonderful undertaking will benefit many beings, and I am so glad to have the information made available in such a way.

Yesterday you were working on an individual practice for breathing to each chakra. We have done a similar practice with a partner, but you were adapting it as a solo practice for use in spiritual occasions. It can be done at the beginning of meditation, as you experimented with this morning. In doing so you felt how it supported you dropping more quickly into a deep and still space. Similarly, it can be done in a group setting, such as the one you were envisioning yesterday of a guided meditation during a spiritual gathering, where it will be even more powerful because of the multiple numbers of people engaging it simultaneously. It will also be quite bonding for the group.

157

You were wondering this morning if this chakra breathing practice could be incorporated into Tantra occasions. My response is "most definitely." Do not be fooled by its simplicity into thinking it is too elementary or only for beginners. It is a powerful and effective practice. As you know, often the most powerful things are very simple. Simplicity is an attribute of truth and therefore of power.

Now we continue. I wish to travel once again to the Sea of Galilee to cleanse your energy body, along with the rest of your being, in the purity we contact there. Take my hand and come with me as we easily course through the ethers to find ourselves once again on the waters at Galilee. We come to rest on the surface, walking on the waves, feeling the soothing rhythm, breathing the refreshing air, suspended easily on the water's lilting swells, carried into the nurturing liquid of life at this sacred location, heart opened to the love of Yeshua that we both carry within our cellular memory, mind opened to the light of God. Drink it in, dear one, and know that it is always here for you.

Let us return to our subject of sacred sexuality. You have completed the first level, in terms of mastering the skills of raising and lowering the sexual energy (also known as life force or sekhem) along the central column of the spine and through all the chakras. Of course, you have been a master of this for quite some time, but now you have completed the first level with Tony. And the sign of this is his enthusiasm for engaging the practice, which is evidence of his full connection to the energy released in this pathway and it making its connections with his various chakras and energy centers.

You can go further in your explorations together by engaging this pathway more before you are physically joined and during your time of intercourse. And you both can continue to slow down the timing in your lovemaking, which will open you both to great wonders of cosmic exploration. Connecting with various aspects of the cosmos is part of the pleasure and magnificence of sacred sexuality. It is not the ultimate point, however, so you do not want to be detoured by becoming a

seeker—in your day you might call it a "groupie"—of this kind of experience. Still, when it occurs it is to be fully honored and received.

Once you have mastered the basic pathway of moving the sexual
energy up and down the central channel, you are ready to learn more
complex patterns. You had one occur spontaneously in your last lovemaking occasion, where you experienced the energy going up to the
crown on your inhalation, down to the root chakra and genitals on the
exhalation, and from there you both orgasmed, which caused the
energy to create a new channel between you that rose up like a foun-
tain. This is indeed one of the energy patterns you can practice at the
intermediate level.

You have also explored another intermediate-level energy pattern,
and this, too, can be engaged during sexuality. It is to breathe the energy
up from the base of the spine to the heart on an inhalation, then retain
the breath as you move the energy through intention in a loop out the
back of the heart, outside the physical body, up the back, curving over
the crown of the head, then coming down the front of the body and
back to the heart. At this point, slowly exhale and move the energy
down through the solar plexus, then the sacral and root chakras. This
heart-looping practice is good to do any time you want to bring more
energy to the heart and the lower chakras. Alternating it with the practice of running energy up to the crown and down to the root can be
especially beneficial and balancing as the latter practice tends to move
the energy upward while the heart-looping practice is more strengthening for the heart and lower chakras. The two work together very well.

The pattern of energy flow in the heart-looping practice has been
compared to the shape of an Egyptian ankh, and indeed that is part of
the derivation of this practice. However, it is not the ultimate meaning
behind the ankh shape, as the ankh is a sacred-geometry symbol used
in the mystery schools in the practices of death and rebirth that are
associated with ascension.[1]

I will give you a third sexual-energy pathway you can now explore *in your lovemaking, which is simple but powerful, too. To begin, come to rest in your sexual connecting and breathe in an alternating fashion, with one partner inhaling while the other exhales. As you do this, keep your mouths very close, as if almost in a kiss, so that you are exchanging breath and life force. This practice is perfect for occasions when you have become very active and want to balance yourselves with more stillness.*

You and Tony have already mastered many steps at the intermediate level. For instance, you have been working to open your throat chakra in your sexual occasions. Tony has learned to have non-ejaculatory orgasms and multiple orgasms? You both are quite developed in your sensitivity to energy and ability to communicate it through touch to your partner. And you both are quite harmonized energetically as a couple and able to easily follow, play with, and merge into each other's energy field. Your level of mastery in this area is uncommon in your time. When you are helping others learn these practices, you will need to support them in all of these areas.

I love you and bless you in your development and service through this work.

I AM Mary Magdalene

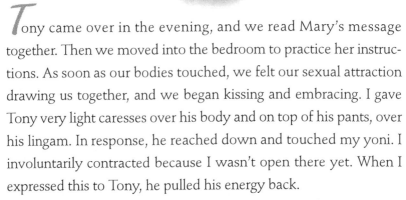

*T*ony came over in the evening, and we read Mary's message together. Then we moved into the bedroom to practice her instructions. As soon as our bodies touched, we felt our sexual attraction drawing us together, and we began kissing and embracing. I gave Tony very light caresses over his body and on top of his pants, over his lingam. In response, he reached down and touched my yoni. I involuntarily contracted because I wasn't open there yet. When I expressed this to Tony, he pulled his energy back.

From there we seemed to get more and more disconnected. I

tried to continue the flow we'd been in earlier, but I couldn't feel a connection with Tony's root chakra. I told him this and we tried various breathing and opening practices, but nothing seemed to work. Finally I said, "It seems like we're trying too hard." Then I added, "Did you get hurt when I said I wasn't ready to be touched at my yoni?"

"I think that must be what happened," he responded. He paused and then offered, "I'm feeling performance anxiety."

We were both surprised to hear that because performance anxiety was not at all typical of Tony. In fact, Tony was one of the most relaxed and accepting people I'd ever known, both of himself and others. "I don't think it's from this lifetime," he said. "I think it's something I'm carrying from a previous incarnation." Having so recently gone through my own healing from a trauma imposed in a previous life, I found it fascinating that now Tony would likewise be purifying from a limiting belief he'd been carrying from a prior incarnation.

We simply relaxed and held each other. I felt compassion for him, without thinking I'd done anything wrong or bad. I also felt grateful that he was able to be so transparent about what was coming up for him. I trusted the process we were going through and was curious about where it would lead.

Eventually we dozed off. I woke up at one point and turned off the light. Then I went back to sleep, happy to be close to Tony. The next thing I knew, he was stirring and breathing strongly next to me. He was still asleep and lying on his back, but his body was moving in a very exaggerated Tantric wave motion. With each inhalation, his body arched so strongly that his neck and shoulders lifted off the bed; on the exhalation, his body curved so forcefully in the other direction that he seemed to be spasming. This continued over and over again.

I whispered in Tony's ear, "What's happening?"

He gently came to consciousness and said, "I was receiving divine light. I'd been praying for this." The fact that he not only heard my whisper but that it immediately brought him to waking consciousness struck me as very unusual, because Tony is hard of hearing and can rarely hear me when I speak softly. His answer surprised me as well because he spoke it in a matter-of-fact way as though he'd been participating in an everyday occurrence. But it certainly didn't seem like that to me.

I wasn't feeling the energy Tony was experiencing. It was uniquely his and very powerful. I moved toward him, and he put out his arm to embrace me as the movements continued. I began to move with him, inhaling and exhaling in sync. Each time the energy moved down to our root chakras, we exploded in energetic orgasms. The energy seemed electric, almost as though there were sparks flying. Now I was able to feel the experience, too, and it was potent.

Eventually we came to rest. Then I turned over, and Tony embraced me in the spoon position. After a while, he began stroking me, and I drew him inside me effortlessly, moving into lovemaking that was both powerful and loving. The connection was quite strong now, completely different from our earlier experience. Tony told me, "This is like a dream."

We came to rest again and were silent for some time. Then he said, "Do you see that?"

I didn't see anything. "What are you seeing?" I asked him.

"I see a very large orb by the door.[3] It's changing colors and moving around, almost as though it's dancing." He paused, and then went on. "There's more than one—two or three." He paused again, then said euphorically, "Now I see many more! There are orbs all over the room, and they're changing colors."

I put on my glasses but still couldn't see them. Even so, I had no doubt that Tony could. Eventually I relaxed toward sleep, and as I closed my eyes I could feel the energy of the orbs, although I never saw them. They were very joyful, a little playful, and amused. I sensed they were excited and happy about the energy that Tony and I were exploring and came to check it out. Then I fell asleep.

Tony stayed awake for another hour, enjoying the display. Eventually he drifted off, too.

I woke in the morning to see Tony quietly getting out of bed. He was trying to leave without disturbing me so I could sleep in. When he saw I was up, he came back to bed and we entwined our bodies around each other, happy to be together and amazed by the night's events. Soon we were making passionate love, blissfully expressing our intimacy and bondedness.

Figure 25-1. ANKH BREATHING PRACTICE
Also described as the heart-looping practice

1. On an inhalation, breathe the sexual energy up from the base of your spine to your heart.

2. While retaining the breath, use your intention to move the energy in a loop out the back of your heart, outside your physical body, up your back, curving over the crown of your head, then coming down the front of your body and back to your heart.

3. Slowly exhale and move the energy down through your solar plexus, then your sacral and root chakras.

Figure 25-2. OPPOSITION BREATHING PRACTICE

1. Come to rest in your sexual connecting.

2. Breathe in an alternating fashion, with one partner inhaling while the other exhales. Have your mouths very close, as if almost in a kiss, so that you are exchanging breath and life force.

Figure 25-3.
ADDITIONAL INTERMEDIATE-LEVEL PRACTICES

FOR WOMEN: Fully connect with your sexual energy, and open your throat chakra in sexual occasions.

FOR MEN: Learn to have nonejaculatory orgasms and multiple orgasms.

FOR WOMEN AND MEN:

- Develop sensitivity to energy and the ability to communicate it through touch to your partner.

- Harmonize energetically as a couple and learn to follow, play with, and merge into each other's energy field.

TWENTY-SIX

Timing

*T*hree days later, Tony and I had plans to go to a tango practice party. Tony was still taking beginning classes, while I was continuing at the intermediate level. This was to be our first time dancing tango together.

I wore a skirt I'd recently bought and was saving for a special dance event. Cut very short in the front, it tapered down to full length at the back. I wore it with shiny black leggings and felt very sexy.

I arrived at the studio before Tony and started socializing with friends. Periodically I'd look toward the door, hoping to see Tony and a little nervous that he might not come, as had occurred before. Recognizing that my old limiting belief of "I'm not loved" was in full swing, I practiced not feeding it. Nevertheless, my heart leapt when Tony finally came through the door. He told me he really liked what I was wearing, and I drank in his appreciation, glowing with delight.

The party started with a lesson from a very accomplished tango teacher. He and his dance partner gave an exquisite demonstration of tango, looking smooth and connected. Then he began guiding us.

Tony and I danced the first dance together and decided to stay together even when the teacher instructed us to change partners.

We were trying out the moves, finding our rhythm together, and thoroughly enjoying expressing our intimacy in this form. It was a deeply bonding experience. Even though Tony had just begun learning tango, he already had a natural feeling for it. But it was more than just his technical ability. I was dancing with someone I loved! That changed everything. Our hearts were engaged and our bodies were following. It was exquisite!

Eventually the DJ started interspersing other dance music between the tango selections. Tony and I danced most of those, too. When he didn't know the dance, I taught him, impressed at how quickly he picked them all up. I knew he was a good dancer from our freestyle dancing at the blues club we sometimes went to, but I wasn't sure how he'd deal with the more structured social dances. I discovered he was just as good at those, which pleased me, since dance is such an important part of my life.

Afterward we came back to my place and shared some thoughts about our Tantric exploration. I'd had an informal communication from Mary earlier that day, in which she gave a simple direction for us, explaining that we were doing well with the Tantric energy practices before and after our lovemaking, and our next step was to integrate them, especially the Tantric wave, into our lovemaking itself.

"Mary has acknowledged that we're in the intermediate phase, where we'll be going deeper and encountering new challenges," I explained as we sat on my bed. "I think we're at a place in our sexuality that's similar to the transition in a relationship from the honeymoon phase to the commitment phase. All of a sudden the relationship starts to feel a little more trying. You become aware of the snags, or 'blah' spots. I think what's really going on is that we've let each other in closer to our core so new issues tend to surface. I trust that if we go through this phase together, it will bring us even closer, along with bringing growth and healing to both of us."

We began to hold and kiss each other, intending to bring more of the energy practices into our lovemaking. We went more slowly than usual, which didn't feel as spontaneous or easy as our sexual occasions in the past. But we stuck with it, willing to explore and experience this, too.

Tony felt particularly challenged by the slow speed at which we were moving, finding that he wasn't getting aroused as easily as before. We talked about how we have different natural rhythms, with mine being slower and his being faster, discussing how we might harmonize our timing. Again, we didn't really have the "answer" and were OK with being in the unknown for now.

I, too, noticed a change, which I'd been increasingly aware of during our last few intimate occasions. It was becoming almost impossible for me to make love physically without first feeling the energetic connection. Until I experienced our energies blending and moving together, I seemed to be in limbo, waiting for something to happen that brought me to life. I'd become especially sensitive to this at the moment when Tony would first enter me. If I only felt the physical penetration, it was as though I was being pushed into, a sensation I did not enjoy.

We experimented with breathing together just before Tony entered me. With his lingam poised lightly right at the entrance to my yoni, we inhaled and exhaled all the way through our genitals and into each other's our bodies. As I opened to his lingam, I felt like he was riding a wave of liquid energy into my yoni. It was exceedingly pleasurable.

Our loving became extremely intense, leading to a powerful extended orgasm for both of us. When we came to rest, Tony told me he'd ejaculated, which he almost never does. "I think it's because it's so late and I'm tired," he suggested before heading home. However, I thought it had more to do with the way the practices had opened us up more deeply, and perhaps the relief of finding our connection after a challenging start. Whatever the cause may have been, we were clearly getting our bearings at a new level of vulnerability.

I woke up the next morning thinking about Tony's and my preferences for different kinds of physical touch. I liked slow touch with light pressure, while Tony enjoyed faster touch with stronger pressure. Yet in spite of these differences, I could remember countless times when we'd powerfully connected. Clearly there was more involved than just the physical. I started to see that Mary was helping us shift from a more conventional lovemaking style, where people stimulate each other physically in order to build energy, to a Tantric approach, where people connect energetically first and then *follow* the flow of energy with their bodies, allowing it to initiate and direct the movement. It's like the difference between steering a motorboat through water and surfing the waves.

During my ten years in Hawaii I had watched many surfers hanging out in the water, often for considerable periods of time, waiting for the right wave to carry them to shore. Hearing many of them describe what it felt like to ride a really good wave, I learned the wait was worth it for the high they experienced. The same is true of Tantra, I now concluded. You have to let go of leading with the physical body and allow the energy body to take over. The best way to support that shift is to relax the physical body, even to the point of stillness, and tune in to energy in much the same way that a surfer, floating on the water, tunes in to the waves.

Excited by the clarifying aspects of this analogy, I slipped out of bed and wrote this note to myself:

> Breathing fully amplifies the connection to energy, as do relaxed movements of the pelvis and spine that follow the breath. Eventually the energy takes over, just like a great wave

carrying a surfer. At that point, you may be led to move faster or in all kinds of ways in response to the rising energy. Your breath may quicken, too. But you can still keep your breath and your body relaxed, allowing the energy to move through you while at the same time moving you. When the energy subsides, you can once again return to stillness or one of the Tantric energy practices until the next "wave" of energy comes along and carries you to new heights of ecstasy.

A good way to deepen your energetic connection to your partner is to remain fully in your energy body throughout the day. Then when you come together for sexuality, there won't be a big shift to go through, since you'll already be experiencing the integration of your physical and energy bodies. You simply extend it to your lovemaking.

When I went to my computer, I received this message from Neale Donald Walsh: "On this day of your life, dear friend, I believe God wants you to know . . . that life begins at the end of your comfort zone." It seemed to apply perfectly to my lovemaking with Tony.

Later I sent Tony a text that read:

When I saw you come in the door at the dance party, I felt really excited and pleased. There you were! And I was delighted that you liked what I was wearing. Thinking about all that, I am full of love and desire for you. I feel you energetically in my yoni. I wish you were here with me now and we were making love.

TWENTY-SEVEN

Loveseat

I woke up two mornings later feeling fantastic. While savoring a cup of green tea, I prepared for a telephone interview. Tony texted me, sending his love and blessings for the call. The interview went fantastically well.

Tony called around noon, and I shared my good news with him. We decided to get together and go hiking, as it was a perfect fall day. As we were driving to our favorite hiking trail, Tony asked me, "How is your yoni doing? I've been concerned about you."

To my delight, I wasn't feeling any unusual sensations there at all, just the quietness of a content yoni. Tony said, "I feel very relieved to hear that. I was afraid I was causing you pain."

"I felt like it was our size differential, not you," I replied. "But even that doesn't make sense because we're such a wonderful fit when we're making love. I've come to think I don't need to analyze it. It's enough for me that I healed my belief and released an entity, and now I'm different. Hallelujah!"

Being outdoors was exhilarating and calming, all at the same time. When we finished our hike, Tony asked, "What would you like to do now?"

Without a moment's hesitation, I answered, "I'd like to teach you the rest of my meditation practice."

"I'm up for that. Let's go to my place. My housemate's away, and it will be private and quiet there."

After arriving at Tony's house, I reviewed the entire practice with him. When we were ready to get started, Tony asked, "Would you lead the meditation out loud?"

"I could for the first part," I offered, "but the second half is a progression, and as each stage is activated everyone proceeds at their own pace. So you'll be on your own for that part."

We started and, like everything we did together, it felt easy and enriching. I effortlessly moved into the meditation and enjoyed it a great deal, especially since I hadn't meditated in several days. When I brought the meditation to a close, Tony said, "I feel like we only just began. It felt so short." In fact, we'd probably been meditating for twenty minutes or longer. "I was traveling far, far out into the cosmos," he added. "I could have stayed there a long time."

"I'd love to connect our sexual energy now in the *yab-yum* position," I told Tony (see figure 27-1).[1] "We've never done that before. We can do it with our clothes on." Tony was happy to oblige me.

Tony sat on the loveseat, which we decided was appropriately named, and I positioned myself on his lap with my legs wrapped around him. Gazing into each other's eyes, we began doing the Tantric wave, undulating our bodies together as we breathed our energy up and down our spines. I suggested a variation for the exhalation portion of the wave—breathing our exhaled energy down to our genitals and then continuing, through each other's genitals, all the way to each other's heart. This variation intensified our connection and we both deeply enjoyed our exchange. We agreed to try it next time with full intercourse.

Figure 27-1. YAB-YUM POSITION

TWENTY-EIGHT

Orgasmatron

*T*wo nights later was our next tango class. I was stressed when Tony picked me up because I was worried we were going to be late. Tony, for his part, was tired from a long day of work on a home remodeling job he was doing. Concerned about the lack of connection between us I said, "I want to talk about what I'm feeling so I can release it. I'm stressed from leaving later than we agreed to and worried that we'll miss the first part of class."

"I think we should drive separately in the future," Tony offered.

Reluctant to give up spending time together beforehand and arriving together, I suggested, "What if, when we have an engagement, you were to call me anytime you're running late. Then I could drive myself." That felt good to both of us, and as I relaxed I felt my openness with Tony return. But I could still feel his tiredness.

We each took our own tango class and then decided to take a second class together. It felt great to be dancing with Tony. Afterward he commented, "You sure get energized by dancing!" He was right. Dancing consistently brings me joy and lifts me up, no matter how low I feel beforehand.

We came back to my house, where we reviewed some of my latest writing describing our implementing Mary's instruction. Tony commented, "It's amazing how reading it together brings back all the feelings of our experience." I agreed. By the time we'd finished, we both were feeling turned on. Moving to the loveseat, I sat on Tony's lap in the yab-yum position and began massaging his neck to help him relax from his hard day at work. He responded with moans of pleasure and release. "I didn't realize how much tension I was holding from all the lifting I'd done today," he said.

"Would you like me to massage your back?" I asked. He readily accepted.

We moved to the bed so Tony could lie down and fully relax. I massaged him for quite a while, working the kinks out of the tight areas and feeling his energy start to flow again. Eventually the massage turned into kissing and then holding each other, and before long we were making love. Tony entered me from behind, a position I love, and our exchange became very charged as waves of bliss ran through me.

After a while we came to rest, transported and thoroughly satisfied. Tony, holding me in our resting position, said, "I really treasure this part of our loving, where we hold each other and bask in our merged energies and heart-space."

"Do you remember what you said the other night?" I asked, laughing with amusement. "You described the ecstatic realm we enter in our sexuality as an orgasmatron."

Tony laughed with me, then added, "My tiredness has vanished. I feel full of energy now." He paused, then continued, "I feel so thankful to Mary for guiding us into the most amazing lovemaking I've ever experienced." I shared his sentiments.

TWENTY-NINE

Sensitivity

*I*t had been three days since I'd seen Tony, and I woke up with my heart hurting. He'd said he would call but hadn't. Our only contact had been a quick text exchange before I went to bed two nights before.

The next day was our one-year anniversary—and also the last day I could spend with Tony before leaving for Austin with my daughter and celebrating my birthday there. We'd talked about celebrating our anniversary but hadn't made specific plans. I began to feel hurt, sad, and alone. The lump in my throat was growing by the minute, with tears right behind. Then it occurred to me to ask Mary for help. I went to my altar and reached out to her. Her response was immediate.

Dear one,

Blessings to you.

You are in pain right now and have called on me. I've come to you to help you.

My dear sister, I am enfolding you in my arms and holding you. It is safe for you to drop into your feelings, to experience them fully, and to express them, just as a young child does naturally.

You are in pain because of feeling alone when you want to be close, and it is Tony in particular you want to be close to. You have not had the contact with him you desire over the last few days. You are also moving into a time when you have expectations regarding your anniversary and birthday, as well as the upcoming trip to meet your mother and stepfather. All of this is combining to create great sensitivity and vulnerability in you. What you need to do is to express this to Tony. Let him see and feel your vulnerability. Help him understand why you have the feelings you do.

You are correct in your awareness that your sensitivity is unusual amongst people on Earth at this time. It is not unusual for higher-dimensional beings, but that is not who you are interacting with on the physical plane. You are different from most, and most find you difficult to understand. They do not, in general, have the ability to understand you on their own because you are ahead of them in terms of capabilities. That is why it is up to you to help others understand you. This will not only benefit you; it will also support the people you interact with in their learning and growth, giving them insight into what's possible and, in fact, what is already the case at levels they do not tend to be conscious of.

Do not think there is something wrong or bad with you for being the way you are. There are many things about you that others enjoy and are attracted to. Nonetheless, it is difficult and often lonely to be different from others.

Do not hold back in your heart. Express yourself with care and love. Do not overwhelm others with your feelings, but do not hold back either.

This is essential for your well-being. When you hold back your feelings, they build up in you and you become unhappy, closed down, and disconnected from Source. Do not allow this, for it is destructive for you.

Mercedes: Is there something about my birthday that brings up pain for me?

Yes, that is a good insight. There is an imprint in you convincing you that you will be abandoned and unloved on your birthday. This is from a subconscious memory dating back to your birth and associated with your father. You did not feel wanted by your father because he had hoped for a boy rather than a girl. This painful memory is restimulated each year just before your birthday. So you need healing and perhaps reassurance from your partner at this time.

Remember your Source. Remember your connection to God and your strength in that. Mourn your pain, but do not put it onto others. Express your hurt, but take responsibility for it. You always have the ability to care for yourself. And you are strong, much stronger than you realize.

I love you and bless you. I stand for you and with you.

In love,
I AM Mary Magdalene

*R*eflecting on Mary's reminder that I could care for myself, I thought about taking myself to Ojo Caliente Mineral Springs Resort & Spa, about an hour north, the next day. The thought made me feel both nurtured and sad, as this was something Tony and I had talked about doing together to celebrate my birthday.

Tony came over later that afternoon. I was able to tell him that I was upset and why. "I'm sorry I didn't call," he said. "It won't happen again." He went on to describe the work he'd been doing to remodel his plant room. I was confused because I thought he was planning to sell his house as a step toward our living together at some point in the future. I asked him about this, and he said, "I'm still planning to do that. I can take the plants with me when I move." To me, it seemed like a lot of energy to be putting into a house that was going to be sold.

Then he said, "I'm going to have dinner with my daughter and her family tonight. Would you like to come?"

"I don't know," I said hesitantly. Normally I enjoyed spending time with his grandchildren, but in that moment I felt confused about what I wanted.

"OK. I'll call later to see how you feel. Would you like me to give you a kiss before I go?"

"No," I said, "I don't."

But as he was leaving, I called him back and asked, "Did you want to kiss me?"

"Of course I did, or I wouldn't have asked you."

"It makes a difference for me to hear you say you want to kiss me," I told him, "rather than asking if I want to kiss you."

"I want to kiss you," he told me. "Would you like to kiss?"

I checked in with myself and realized I was torn. A part of me did and a part of me didn't. I told Tony that and could see the pain in his eyes. I didn't know what else to do. He left, looking dejected.

I pondered my options. Since Tony had made his plans for dinner without me, I decided to have my own fun without him. I called Audrey, and we agreed to a girl's night, with a movie and popcorn at my house. Before the movie, we talked about what was going on with Tony and me. Audrey commented poignantly, "It seems like Tony is giving you enough to keep you involved but not giving you what you really want." I reluctantly agreed with her perspective.

Tony called close to 10:00 p.m. and left a message inviting me to dinner and a soak at the local spa the next evening. I was touched by his invitation but didn't feel moved to do either. I texted him back, saying, "Thanks for the invitation. I think I'm going to Ojo tomorrow." Neither of us mentioned our anniversary.

THIRTY

Community

The next day I woke up feeling calm and looking forward to going to Ojo Caliente. I began working, thinking I only had a few things to attend to, and soon found myself immersed in several projects.

Around midmorning I decided to take a break and read a chapter in the online book I'd started about the secrets of relating to men. This section focused on women's erroneous assumptions about men—that they're lazy, stubborn, clueless, self-centered, and so forth, as well as women's tendencies to judge both men and themselves against an impossible standard of perfection. I considered to what extent I had done that with Tony the day before.

By the time I finished reading the chapter, I felt open in my heart. I decided to text Tony to see if he wanted to go to Ojo with me.

I was pleased and excited when I received his response: "I'd love to go with you!"

The early afternoon flew by, and I seemed to need every minute of it for accomplishing the work I'd set out to do. Before I knew it, Tony was at the door. We shared a warm hug and kiss, and then took off. The drive to Ojo was spectacular, with the last golden colors of the aspens fluttering in the wind like rivers of warm sunlight. We drove with the sunroof open and caught up with each other on what we'd been doing since yesterday afternoon. I felt very relaxed and, surprisingly, turned on.

When we arrived at the hot springs, I told Tony, "On the drive here, I wished we were making love."

"I was feeling that, too," he confided.

It had been twenty years since Tony had last been at Ojo, and he was impressed with the many changes that had occurred at this largely undeveloped natural hot springs. Now it was a beautiful spa, which had been aesthetically designed in the old New Mexico style, deeply resonating with the natural feeling and sacredness of the earth.

We changed into our swimsuits and met each other at the first cliffside pool, where iron-rich water bubbled up from beneath the soft natural-gravel base. As I descended the steps, my body melted into the delicious warm water. I glided over to where Tony was waiting and continued melting into his body and lips. The sun was setting, and the crescent moon was shining above us. All was well in the world.

A group of women were talking animatedly on one side of us. On the other side were several couples enjoying the ambiance. We silently held each other, kissing and feeling our bodies effortlessly merging, supported by the soothing water. It felt liberating to so freely express our intimacy in the presence of others. Tony sat on a ledge in the water, and I sat on his lap in the yab-yum position, my legs wrapped around him. Eventually we stood up and did a little tango together, moving slowly through the liquid warmth.

We fluidly progressed to the second pool, a larger enclosed soda-spring pool. Here we were much more buoyant, which brought out our playfulness. We moved through the water together, almost chasing each other and then coming together, swirling around, enjoying motion that seemed natural, like two dolphins playing together. We moved into a corner and became very still, holding each other close. Without words, we began the Tantric wave, breathing and undulating our energy up and down our spines in unison. Without making a sound, we began to have energy orgasms under the water. I felt my consciousness shifting into the deep state that sexual pleasure takes me into, yet deepened even more by the powerful relaxation of the sensual warm water.

It was getting dark as we transitioned to the third pool, again outdoors, where warm water, strong in arsenic, poured out of a huge earthen jar into one end of the pool. The rock face behind the pool was lit up by spotlights, illuminating various shapes in the crevices of the rock. One looked like a wolf riding a large four-legged creature and another resembled a whale. By now we were so deeply relaxed we were nearly in a trance.

We went into one of the buildings for a drink of lemon water strong in lithium and then decided to try the sauna. After a short time, we were thoroughly melted and realized it was nearly 9:00 p.m. We changed back into our clothes and were delighted to discover that the restaurant was still open. We had an exquisite meal there, every mouthful teeming with the most satisfying flavors. It was the perfect completion to the sensory gratification of our soak.

We drove home struggling to stay awake, singing to the CD of inspirational songs I'd made for Tony. When we got to my house, I asked Tony if he'd like to spend the night, and he said he would.

We'd barely stepped into the bedroom when Tony was kissing me, holding me, and taking off my clothes all at the same time. I loved his excitement and also knew I needed to go slower. Once he had slowed down for me, we found our rhythm easily and moved into magnificent lovemaking.

As we shifted into holding each other, I said, "Happy anniversary."

Tony smiled and answered, "Happy anniversary."

Feeling completely fulfilled, I asked him, "Would you like to spoon to go to sleep?"

"Yes," he said dreamily, and we shifted into that position. Soon we were aroused again and before we knew it we were making love a second time. We had more energy than either of us expected. Finally, out of tiredness, we began to drift off.

I heard Tony say, "Oh my, they're here again."

"What are you talking about?" I mumbled.

"It's the orbs of light. They're back." I reached over and got my glasses. Even before I put them on I could see something I hadn't seen before. The corner of the room by the door was full of light, with some spots brighter than others. But while I had a definite sense of their presence, I still couldn't see distinctive orbs.

Tony said, "They're moving all about and changing colors. They really like our energy when we make love, and they like spending time with us." I could feel their enjoyment, too.

I thought about my journey the year before in Sedona, when I visited the fourth-dimensional beings at the center of the Earth. I remembered them telling me that sexual energy is the way they maintain the fabric of their reality. That idea seemed similar to the way that sunlight supports our third-dimensional reality. I told Tony, "I think they're fourth-dimensional beings. This is the beginning of our community." Then I drifted off to sleep, happy and deeply satisfied.

THIRTY-ONE

Sunlight through Water

*T*hree days later my daughter and I embarked on our road trip to Austin. Tony arrived, as planned, the night before her return flight. I picked him up at the airport around 1:00 a.m., and we went to the hotel room we'd reserved for the two of us. Both tired, we promptly fell into bed. It felt so good to be next to him again. Our bodies and energy merged as we held each other close. Without even trying, our breathing began to harmonize, our energy moving easily up and down our spines. As it flowed into our root chakras, we both experienced light energy orgasms.

Just before we drifted off to sleep, Mary came to me with a very brief message. She told me that our next step was to move beyond the spasms of release we were experiencing, as they were merely discharging tension. Now we were to relax more fully, allowing the pleasure to move through us like sunlight penetrating deeply through a pool of water. I wasn't sure how we would do that, but trusted that Mary would guide us.

Tony and I slept in, happy to have a leisurely morning together and wanting to reconnect sexually. Our bodies easily flowed together, but I didn't feel our energy connecting. Soon we came to stillness with Tony still inside of me, and I asked, "Could we do the sharing process?" Tony happily agreed. We each had a round, mostly communicating our happiness to be physically together again. Tony expressed his appreciation of me and how much he liked my lacy underwear. I still didn't feel any more connected and suspected there was more we needed to say.

Tony had shared briefly the night before that he'd been dealing with his ex-wife's medical care. I guessed he needed to release feelings he was having about that and gently began to explore with him what those might be. He immediately tapped in to irritation he was holding around recent events with her. He expressed his hopeful anticipation of being released from his caretaking role, which he had not enjoyed but had performed with great dependability.

Soon the energy between us was rich and full, and we returned to our lovemaking, with genuine pleasure and excitement. I didn't try to engage Mary's instruction or even share it with Tony yet, but I did ask him to slow down at several points, which he immediately did, taking us into even greater depths of feeling and bliss.

Afterward, Tony commented, "I really liked our slowing down. It felt like we slowed down even more than we have previously." I agreed wholeheartedly. I was especially struck by the freedom I felt in asking for the slower pacing, asserting myself in a way that was new for me in the midst of lovemaking. I attributed my change to Mary's support for me opening my throat chakra and power center. I loved Tony's responsiveness to my suggestions and ideas, and how unthreatened he was by my taking the lead at times. In this I felt his deep sense of inner security, which allowed him to be quite the avid explorer in new realms.

We didn't have as much time as usual since we were meeting my mother and stepfather for lunch, so we ended our intimacy after about forty-five minutes. Moving together like clockwork, we showered, dressed, and took off to meet them, getting lost in the tangle of Austin highways but managing to get to the restaurant just as my mother and stepfather were ordering. It turned out they'd gotten lost on their way to lunch, too. I was amused at the way Spirit seemed to be stretching time for us.

This was the first time Tony had met my mom and stepdad. He commented afterward that he liked my mother a lot, which delighted me. After saying our good-byes, Tony and I took off to explore downtown, retracing the route my daughter and I had traveled the day before. It was especially fun this time because Tony was attuned to the different architectural styles and periods of the buildings, which I had not previously noticed.

"I want to find a really nice restaurant to celebrate your birthday," Tony announced. We stopped at a small eatery called Thai Passion and snuggled next to each other in a booth. We began with wine and two appetizers, followed by delicious entrees and topped off with green tea. The food was mouthwatering good, but our kisses and joy in sharing it were even better. Afterward we walked up and down 6th Street, stopping in a club with a band playing sixties and seventies favorites and having great fun dancing together.

We got lost on the way to our hotel, but neither of us really minded. Eventually we found it and settled into our room, where I checked my email as Tony got ready for bed. By the time I crawled under the covers Tony was fast asleep. Wanting to be close, I snuggled up next to him. To my surprise, he woke up and was fully alert. He gave me a long, sensual back massage, accompanied by my soft moans of pleasure. From there, we very slowly and consciously moved into lovemaking.

As he was about to enter me, I said, "Let's be still and just breathe. I want to feel you breathe into me till our shared breathing draws you inside me." Tony did as I asked, and soon a wave of energy tenderly carried him deep into my inner recesses. We continued our breathing together and our slow pacing, letting our bodies move together in unhurried passion to greater frontiers of ecstasy than we'd experienced before. Our erotic dance had its own rhythms, moving us effortlessly into waves of faster movements, then returning us again to our baseline of deliberate slowness. When we finally came to stillness, I was completely energized and filled with rapture, my entire spine vibrating at a high frequency. I was amazed at our potential for having ever-greater experiences of profound joy and sexual fulfillment. Without my talking to Tony about Mary's instruction of the previous evening, we seemed to have accomplished it.

THIRTY-TWO

Erotic Abandon

I woke up in Tony's arms. Instinctively, I began massaging his neck and back, thoroughly enjoying the sound of his deep moans and the way he melted into my touch. The massage progressed into languorous kissing and stroking, and before long we were making love.

We continued the deep breathing in lovemaking we'd begun the evening before. Sensing the possibility of opening ourselves even further into it, I spontaneously said to Tony, "Breathe me into you," as I did the same to him. Suddenly our lovemaking dropped into a whole new expanse of exquisite sensation. I felt as though I could taste Tony, beginning at his lingam, going through my yoni all the way up into my mouth, and continuing from there to light up the entire crown of my head. The fullness of our exchange was explosive, like a superb fireworks display.

Checking the clock, we discovered it was three minutes after checkout time. Reluctantly, we ended our lovemaking and got ready to leave.

It was a gorgeous fall day in Austin—warm, sunny, and lightly breezy. We went to the original Whole Foods in Austin and enjoyed a sumptuous, slow lunch. Tony wanted to spend the afternoon taking in the city, so we started by visiting a few bookstores, then attended a book festival that was taking place in tents around the capitol building, and ended by exploring the stately capitol building itself, which was filled with Texas history and beautifully maintained. The sun was low when we emerged from the building, so we returned to Whole Foods for a quick dinner and then took off for the first leg of our journey back to Santa Fe.

The drive through West Texas was uneventful, and we both were fighting off fatigue. We played the Austin radio station as long as we could pick up the signal and then shared stories to keep each other awake, trading off driving periodically. We cheered when we pulled into our motel at 12:30 a.m., aware that we couldn't have stayed awake much longer. Once in our room we climbed under the cozy comforter, and before we knew it we were sound asleep.

I woke up to Tony bringing me a cup of fresh-squeezed orange juice from the hotel's breakfast buffet. Then he took off his pants and climbed back into bed. We were both refreshed and happy to be close. Tony gave me a long back massage, working out the kinks in my neck. We were both getting turned on, but I said, "I don't think I should make love because my yoni was sore yesterday evening." Tony agreed, and we talked about how hard it is for us to refrain from connecting sexually as the draw is so strong for us. I also thought that giving up intercourse for a few days might be an opportunity for us to deepen in our energetic exchange.

We continued to stroke each other and our sexual energy became more intense. I asked Tony, "Would you like to take off my panties?" and he happily complied. He then touched my yoni, and I could feel myself subtly pulling back. "The moment I take off my panties is a sensitive transition point for me," I explained. "I suddenly feel more vulnerable and also a little disconnected from all the physical shifting involved in removing my clothing. What I need afterward is to come to rest and reconnect with your energy."

"I know that," Tony said, "but I forget."

"What would help you remember?" I asked him.

"That's an interesting question," he replied. "I don't actually forget; it's just that I get so excited when you're naked that I get overwhelmed with the intensity of my sexual feelings. My body responds before I even realize what I'm doing."

I was touched by his honesty and openness. "Would it help if you breathed the energy up to your heart?" I asked.

"Let's try it." We relaxed into breathing together. "That actually makes a big difference," he reported. "I feel calm and balanced now, while also energized."

"In Tantra, men are often compared to fire," I said. "They're highly combustible and ignite quickly, but also tend to die out quickly. Women, on the other hand, are likened to water, taking much longer to come to boiling, but then maintaining their boiling point for an extended time. In Tantra, it mostly rests with the man to align his energy with the woman's, consciously relaxing his excitement through breathing and slowing down his movements, even including stillness at times. It also helps if he moves the sexual energy up his spine to his heart and crown, and from there spreads it out to his whole body."

I went on to explain the curve of building energy Tantrically in sexual occasions. "Any time a man feels a sense of sexual urgency, especially if it's accompanied by a desire for release, he can intentionally relax his energy—through raising the energy to the higher chakras and spreading it through his body, breathing, and possibly becoming still. This allows him to 'cool down' a bit and stay in sync with his partner. His energy may dip temporarily, and he may also lose a bit of his erection. But I've been told by male Tantricas that their potency quickly returns.

"When the sense of urgency on the man's part has passed and he's once again in harmony with his partner's energy, they can continue to build the energy between them, knowing they can return to the 'relaxation–cool down' phase temporarily whenever they need to. This creates a pattern of building energy, alternating with relaxation, which eventually leads to a much greater movement of sexual energy than most couples experience without this kind of intentional engagement."

I had taught this progression of Tantric arousal in my sacred sexuality workshops, but I'd never explained it to Tony. I was pleased at the way he received it, confident that he was already integrating it. Effortlessly we returned to our physical intimacy. I so loved this about Tony—we could switch gears in virtually any direction with the greatest ease. We didn't seem to get stuck or waylaid.

Our desire for each other turned to passion. Despite our intentions to abstain from intercourse, we soon were making love, simultaneously breathing into each other and breathing the other into ourselves. I trusted that as long as our movement and breathing were connected, I'd be fine.

However, I noticed that when Tony got very excited his movements took the lead and became faster, although he was continuing to breathe in the slow rhythm we were sharing. Because my connection was to his breathing, at those times I felt out of sync with his body. I asked him to pause and suggested, "Let's focus on our energy and breathing, letting our movements follow from those."

What followed seemed absolutely magical. We both completely let go of trying to make anything happen and simply tuned in to our energy and shared breathing. For a brief time we rested in stillness, willing to see what would happen if we totally let go. Suddenly a tremendous wave of ardent sensation picked us up, and we began moving with wild, erotic abandon, carried into surges of sexual bliss. Like a fantastic ride on the ocean's surf, we smoothly came to a peaceful stillness, only to be picked up again by another swell of powerful sexual energy, transporting us to new vistas of euphoric delight. This happened again and again.

Eventually we came to rest, thoroughly satiated and deeply connected. Tony rightly suspected we were once again pushing the limit of checkout time. With one last embrace, we happily transitioned out of bed and into functioning mode as we prepared to resume our drive home.

THIRTY-THREE

Taoist Practice

The next morning, I was delighted to again wake up in Tony's arms. We were staying with a friend in Roswell before the last leg of our trip. Tony gave me a deep massage on my neck and then moved to a sore spot on my back. My pains seemed to melt away. Then I asked him, "Would you like a massage?" He immediately accepted. I started working on his lower back and quickly found a spot that was tightly knotted. I worked on it a long time, asking him to breathe into it with me. Eventually I moved on to the rest of his spine, switching from my fingers to my elbow so I could go as deeply as possible. His moans of release told me it was working.

After a while, I switched to long, flowing strokes over his whole back. I moved down his legs to his feet, massaging all the muscles down to his toes. Then I worked back up to his shoulders and moved down his arms, wrists, palms, and fingers. Finally I massaged his scalp, accompanied by sounds of deep delight from Tony.

We traded roles again, with Tony stroking my back very lightly. My pelvis started moving and circling with him, and I could feel a powerful longing for him deep inside. Guiding his lingam to the entrance of my yoni, he entered me very slowly. We remained still for a few minutes, breathing together. Then we got swept away in a powerful tide of passion. Our lovemaking was strong and unhurried, with faster movements woven in. It felt scrumptious being deeply intertwined, still sharing our breathing and energy.

Our rhythms moved to peaks of bliss, over and over. Even when we stopped, the energy flowing between us remained extremely intense. As we held each other in stillness, Tony said, "I really like breathing our energy into each other and breathing each other's energy back into ourselves."

"That reminds me of a Taoist exercise," I told him, "in which the man thrusts shallowly into the woman nine times, followed by a very deep penetration. There's a variation of that I'd love to try. It starts with engaging nine quick thrusts, with both people exhaling on each one. That's followed by a slow, deep penetration as both partners inhale slowly up to their crown, with an accompanying body arch. They hold the breath briefly at the crown and then exhale and round their bodies, moving the energy down to their genitals and root chakra. We could add to that by breathing in each other's energy on the inhalation and sending our energy out to each other on the exhalation."

We immediately started doing the full pattern and experienced a whole new set of amazing sensations, with electrifying waves moving out from our genitals, engulfing us. We came to rest and repeated the pattern several times, enjoying the sensations fully each time.

Near the end of our lovemaking, I had a vision of how to do the ankh pattern as a partner practice. I wasn't sure if it had come from Mary or from a memory of having done this in my past life as a priestess of Isis. In the pattern, both partners breathe the sexual energy up from their genitals to their heart. From there, they circle the energy out the back of the heart, up and over their head and their partner's head, and come down their partner's back to their partner's heart, entering their partner's heart from the back. Then they bring their energy down from their partner's heart to their partner's genitals, and finally back to their own genitals. I sensed I was being given a preview of our next step in learning the practices of sacred sexuality.

At last we came to rest again, holding each other and nesting. Tony looked at his watch and announced we'd been making love for over two hours. We both laughed, agreeing that it was a perfect way to start the day.

Figure 33-1.
SHALLOW- AND DEEP-THRUSTING TANTRIC WAVE
Contributed by Mercedes Kirkel

1. Engage nine quick, shallow thrusts, exhaling together with each one.

2. Begin a slow, deep penetration as you inhale slowly up to your crown, with an accompanying body arch. Breathe in each other's energy as you inhale.

3. Hold your breath briefly at your crown.

4. Exhale and round your bodies, moving the energy down to your genitals and root chakra. Send energy out to your partner as you exhale.

Figure 33-2. PARTNER ANKH PRACTICE

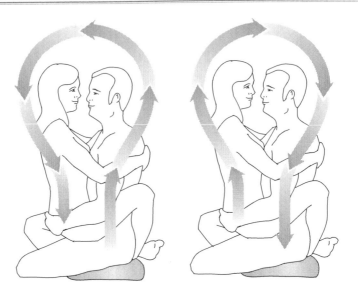

Male Breathing Pattern   *Female Breathing Pattern*

1. Breathe the sexual energy up from your genitals to your heart.

2. Retain the inhaled breath as you move the energy in a loop, bringing it out the back of your heart, up and over your head and your partner's head, down your partner's back to your partner's heart, and entering your partner's heart from the back.

3. Slowly exhale as you bring your energy down your partner's spine, from their heart to their genitals.

4. Briefly rest with your breath fully exhaled as you bring the energy from your partner's genitals back to your own genitals.

THIRTY-FOUR

Phantoms in the Night

We arrived home from our trip the night before Halloween. I felt sad climbing into bed alone and woke up missing the warmth of Tony's body. I also felt overwhelmed by all the work I was coming home to. I made a conscious choice to meditate before diving into it, and was very happy to reconnect with Mary and receive a new message from her.

Blessings and greetings, my beloved one,

Welcome home—both to your home in Santa Fe and, even more, the home in your heart, where I connect with you. This is a timeless, spaceless place. Actually it's more accurate to say it's beyond time and space as you know them.

You are tired, my dear one, and it is good that you have prioritized coming home to your heart through your meditation practice. That is your greatest help, always. Part of the reason you are tired is that you have slipped from abiding in your heart, which is what truly nourishes and sustains you. You must become stronger in your ability to abide continuously in your heart. Becoming overinvolved in your work and worrying about your work take you out of the heart space. You must adapt your emotional disposition toward your work so that it supports your ability to abide in the heart. Staying in the heart must be your priority, and all else in your life must support that.

This is why, in the past, I have spoken so extensively about people's relationship to their emotions—because emotions are one of your greatest allies for staying in your heart. I offered the instruction I did to help people in this most direct pathway of staying in their heart. Unfortunately most people don't realize this and don't make use of their emotions to support themselves.

You must be in your heart space to be able to engage in these sacred sexuality practices. There is a progression to this development, which is necessary because of the way humans are designed and the way they function. It is not something you can bypass.

Ideally, children would learn this way of relating to emotions as they grow up, first by having it modeled to them by the adults around them, and later through direct instruction in how to do it themselves. Children can learn these emotional practices from the age of seven or so. By the time they're teenagers and their sexual energy is emerging, they could be instructed in working with it in the ways we are doing now. Initially it would not be through engaging a partner sexually but simply as a solo practice.

Right now most teenagers do not receive guidance in how to work with this energy, which is unfortunate as it would help them be much more balanced and healthy, both emotionally and energetically. It would help them feel there is nothing bad, dirty, or unacceptable about their sexuality. And it would help them channel their sexual energy in ways that are most supportive of their relational life, their spiritual life, and their eventual sexual life. As your society becomes more enlightened and conscious, this kind of instruction will be provided for young people.

You did not receive this kind of instruction as you were developing or even during most of your adult life. So now, as an adult, you have had to unlearn certain patterns and learn others. You largely escaped the indoctrination that sexuality is evil, sinful, shameful, or tainted. You've seen this as fortunate in your case, but it was not an accident.

It was part of your soul design—something for you to use in carrying out the work you have chosen as a soul. It is the work of the Sacred Feminine, and you have been engaged in it for many, many lifetimes, specifically in the domain of sacred sexuality. You became aware of this as your life purpose about fifteen years ago, but only now are you stepping fully into this calling. The design was already set and clear, and all is unfolding as it should.

This is why you do not need to worry or try to figure out how to "make" things happen, including bringing my teaching to people you sense could be helped by it. It will not happen in that way. The "physics" of this process is different from what you think, and trying to direct it can in fact obstruct its emergence while also operating against your own growth and development.

Your effort, which is really more a kind of intention and awareness, should be to stay attuned to your guidance and to let yourself be directed by that. You are already doing this to a large degree. The places you must now apply it are the arenas in which you are still tending to worry or let yourself get out of balance, such as book marketing. Your growing edge is to let yourself trust in God in those areas.

You are doing so well, my sweet sister, in your relationship with Tony and your engagement of the sexual practices I am giving you. You accurately received the message at the end of your recent lovemaking occasion about the practice of the Egyptian ankh in sexual partnership. You were wondering if this message came from me or from your remembering. I want to clarify that it was from your remembering. This is a very good sign that your memory is awakening. This memory is stored in your causal body, where the soul memory resides.[1] Through your sacred sexuality practices, you are opening to your causal body, a sign that you are being carried into the higher dimensions, where you have much more direct access to your soul memories. You may continue to have memories arise through your sacred sexuality practices as well as understandings you mastered in previous lives.

The veil of forgetting at the third-dimensional level has caused you to "forget" most of what you knew and experienced previously. But throughout your life there has been a bleed-through of your soul memories from prior incarnations. All people have this bleed-through from previous lifetimes, though most aren't consciously aware of it or in acceptance of it. It is why people have talents that they can't explain. Bringing forth gifts and abilities from previous lives is really quite a natural process, but the process of "forgetting" that individuals go through in incarnating into the third dimension makes it seem very mysterious.

Your next step is to engage the partner ankh practice, which you remembered [see figure 33-2]. I trust you will do this at the right moment, when you and your partner are ready.

In the meantime, stay balanced. Prioritize residing in your heart. Stay attuned to your guidance, especially with regard to what actions to take. Have fun. Stay rested. Continue to dance, for expressing your divinity through dance is part of your soul path. It is also helping you learn how to incarnate the Goddess energy and where your limits are in doing that.

I love you and bless you, and thank you for all that you are doing.

In greatest love,
I AM Mary Magdalene

*M*ary's instruction to me to relax my efforts in trying to make things happen was both relieving and somewhat mystifying. It stayed with me strongly throughout the day.

Tony and I had plans to see each other at 5:00 p.m., before his church-group meeting and before the trick-or-treaters would start arriving at my door. I dressed up in a witchy-gypsy outfit, with lots of face and body glitter, including a glitter star on my forehead. Tony arrived precisely at 5:00, and after a passionate kiss, I told him, "I want to jump in bed with you!"

"Me, too!" he readily agreed.

"But I'm not going to because I want to be here to answer the door for the children as they come around."

"Well, then," Tony mused with a smile, "I guess I'll have to come back later." I dusted Tony's face with sparkle and he took off for his group.

I had great fun interacting with the costumed children who came for their Halloween treats, and the time passed quickly till Tony returned. We were both hungry by then and decided to go out for dinner. We ended up at Cowgirl restaurant, where everyone seemed to be sporting costumes.

By the time we got home it was late, but we still had lots of energy. The evening was chilly, so we took off our clothes and snuggled under the covers of my bed. We held each other and began to engage sexually, but I didn't feel our energy connection. I initiated the sharing process, telling Tony, "I've missed being with you after our five days of travel together." His sharing was similar. Feeling more connected, we returned to engaging each other intimately, but something was still off. We focused on breathing together for a while, but it didn't seem to be connecting us. Tony was stroking me in ways that had felt wonderful in the past few days, yet now I wasn't enjoying it.

Finally, we acknowledged that we'd been trying too hard and gave up. I felt frustrated and disappointed. Then Tony went home, and I was left with an achy sadness, wondering what phantoms had come between us.

I woke up the next morning still feeling dismal. It seemed to hang over me all day like a heavy blanket. Tony didn't call or text, and I didn't really want to communicate with him. I was sinking into despair. Finally in the afternoon, I decided to turn my energy around through engaging the practices that connect me to my heart and to God. It wasn't easy, but it felt good.

That evening there was a costume dance party at the dance studio. Tony and I had planned on going, but now I doubted that he would want to. I considered passing on it, too, since my energy was so low. But I decided it would be good for me and forced myself to get dressed up. Tony texted me before the event, confirming my hunch: "I'm still working, so I'm not going to make it to the dance tonight." I wasn't surprised.

I had some fun dances at the party, and many people told me I looked beautiful in my gypsy costume. But I still was sad in my heart about the distance I was feeling from Tony.

On the drive home I started to make sense of what was going on. I knew it wasn't a coincidence that our struggle occurred on the first day back from our trip. I started to see that I was feeling more pain than I was aware of about going back to our usual lives. All of a sudden we were living in different places again, engaged in our own activities and only seeing each other periodically. The previous evening, I'd needed space to feel into that reality with Tony but hadn't given it to myself. Instead, I'd tried to be intimate, as though nothing had changed. But really, a lot had changed.

Once I reached this understanding, I felt more peaceful and the sadness receded a bit. I became more aware of the place the sadness was coming from—my longing for close, continuous partnership. To not have that kind of partnership felt like an emptiness inside me. I questioned whether I'd ever have it with Tony. *Maybe we've just come together to engage the practices Mary's been guiding me through,* I told myself.

Then I remembered that Tony had told me he had a fantastic birthday present for me, but he still hadn't given it to me. He said he forgot to bring it on the trip and would give it to me when we got home. When I saw him on Halloween, he said he'd forgotten it again and would bring it tonight. But I didn't see him tonight and wondered if I'd ever receive it. *Maybe he changed his mind and didn't want to give it to me anymore.*

THIRTY-FIVE

Tango

The next day continued to be difficult. I disciplined myself to stay focused on my work, still catching up after being away. I started to prepare emotionally for not spending time with Tony, thinking of activities and people I could keep busy with over the next couple of evenings. I was particularly interested in seeing the movie *Bless Me Ultima*, which had been highly recommended by a good friend.

Tony called in the afternoon. "I'd like to celebrate your birthday tomorrow evening," he said. "Would you like to go see *Bless Me Ultima* and then go out to dinner?" The frozenness of my love for him immediately began to thaw. I felt happy that he still wanted to celebrate my birthday. "I had a plumbing emergency at my house yesterday," he went on to explain. "That's what kept me from coming to the costume party last night. I have to work late tonight, too. But I'd love to see you tomorrow."

I accepted, with a heart already beginning to lighten.

"Good," Tony said. Then he surprised me again, saying, "I'd like to go with you to the tango festival on Sunday, too." I was especially touched by that.

The next day rolled out with more flow and openness, until I received an email from my previous partner. He'd sent a birthday greeting a few days before, which had started us communicating. I realized we were in a familiar cycle, which generally began with him writing after a period of no contact. Once we were communicating, I would start thinking about him—missing my connection with him and remembering my love for him. That would last for a few days, until he would write something that was painful to receive, triggering unhealed memories and patterns from the past.

I decided to explain that it was too upsetting for me to be in touch with him. I said I would like to hold him in my heart as a friend, but I couldn't really engage in communications with him. By then, my earlier joy had morphed into disturbance.

It was now time to get ready for my date with Tony, but our challenges over the last few days had taken a toll, and the emotional chasm between us still hadn't been bridged. On top of that, I was rattled from the interchange with my past partner.

When Tony arrived, I told him I was feeling down. He immediately asked, "Do you still want to go?"

"Yes," I replied, thinking that he, too, was feeling shaky.

The movie was exquisite and extremely powerful. It was based on a true story from the 1940s, taking place in a small New Mexico town. I was deeply moved and affected by the young Hispanic boy's coming-of-age story and his relationship with his elderly grandmother, a shaman-healer who became his mentor. Afterward we sat in Tony's car and shared our feelings about the movie. Tony told me how different characters in the movie had reminded him of his relatives, and I felt like I was getting to know a different side of him.

Before we left, Tony said he wanted to give me something. I knew he was referring to my birthday present. I was feeling raw from the movie and not sure this was the best time for me to receive his gift, but I accepted his choice. He handed me a package, along with a beautiful New Mexico card with a simple message wishing me a happy birthday. In the package was a very unusual blown-glass piece decorated with flowers and hearts and the words "Happy Anniversary" and "Love." It was a very sentimental gesture, and I was quite touched.

Then Tony handed me another package, which had two gifts inside. The first was a silver pocketknife with many different tools that folded out. I was appreciative and a bit amused by Tony's loving response to my challenges with the basic practicalities of life. The second gift was an original painted pot from a local pueblo that was lovely. I felt Tony's consideration of me in this gift, too, as I hardly had any local art that represented the culture of New Mexico.

The three gifts reflected different parts of Tony—his sensitivity and emotional openness in the delicate blown-glass piece that celebrated our love, his practicality mixed with beauty in the attractive knife, and his deep connection with New Mexico and the spirit of the land conveyed by the pot. Nonetheless, I was a little disappointed that the gifts weren't as personal as I would have liked.

At that moment, Tony surprised me with yet another package. As I opened it, I saw the name of a master jeweler we'd met at the International New Age Trade show in Denver four months before. At her booth, Tony had been particularly attracted to a necklace with a striking diamond-cut crystal that had been made into a powerful Goddess piece. The woman had me try it on, and since Tony often gave gifts of jewelry to his daughters I assumed that's what he had in mind. He bought it and said no more about it.

I unwrapped the package, and there was the exquisite necklace. It was so large and beautiful, I struggled to take in that he was actually giving it to me, especially considering the distance I had felt from him over the past few days. I breathed in deeply and did my best to fully receive it. I felt like I'd really need to expand my image of myself as a server of the Goddess to wear this stunning emblem of her.

Tony treated me to a delicious dinner at an Italian restaurant, which we both enjoyed. By the time we returned to my house, it was late. Since we were planning to leave early the next morning for the tango festival in Albuquerque, we said goodnight without trying to spend intimate time. I was relieved. The cumulative events of the day had already stretched me emotionally in so many ways, and I still had emotional clearing to do before I could be fully open with Tony sexually.

We took off for Albuquerque early the next morning so we could visit my dad before the tango festival. It had been two weeks since I'd last spent time with him, and Tony hadn't seen my dad since his birthday in June. When we arrived, my dad was still in bed, which saddened me. He was struggling more to find the words he wanted and kept losing his thoughts in the process. This seemed to confirm my growing sense that he was gradually becoming less present and more confused. While he still enjoyed making jokes, now it was more often in the form of a look or a few quick words. At one point, the aide on duty transferred him from his bed to a wheelchair, a task that had previously required the assistance of two people. I congratulated him on his increased physical capability even while tracking his mental decline, the obvious paradox demonstrating my growing ability to let go and trust God.

After saying our good-byes with lots of hugs and kisses, we headed out for a quick lunch and then over to the tango festival at a beautiful, old New Mexico–style hotel. Inside, the corridors were lined with vendors selling fancy tango shoes and clothing. I made a mental note to come back and shop when we had a break.

I knew the couple that was teaching our class because they run a studio outside of Santa Fe. Their focus was on deeply feeling the dance and connecting through your heart with your partner, which to me felt like a vertical, moving form of Tantra. With very little talk, they quickly had us moving and dancing, but more importantly feeling the essence of tango. Before long we moved into the Argentine style of close embrace.

Tony and I had decided to switch partners, since there's much to be learned by dancing with various people. I enjoyed exploring my ability to engage the form and merge with different people, but once we started to do close embrace I just wanted to be with Tony.

The next time we were together, I told him, "Tony, I just want to be dancing with you in close embrace."

"I feel the same way," he affirmed. "Let's do the rest of the dances together." And that's what we did for the remainder of the class.

During the break, we returned to browse the dazzling wares of the vendors. Tony decided to buy a new pair of dance shoes, while I found an exotic pair of copper metallic pants. "Go ahead and try them on," Tony encouraged me. "Then show me what they look like on." When I came out he was obviously delighted and offered to buy them for me. I felt so loved and beautiful! I thought about wearing them right then and there, but I decided to save them for a special occasion.

Back on the dance floor, it was easy to flow together. Tony was getting very excited through our dance and was having a hard time keeping from kissing and caressing me. I was simply enjoying the feeling of letting go into his embrace and following his movements. At one point the teacher danced with him to give him personal guidance. Afterward I could feel the change in his dancing, appreciating how quickly he learns and what a natural dancer he is. I felt so blessed to be with him.

After the tango festival, we enjoyed a dinner at a northern New Mexican restaurant before beginning the drive back to Santa Fe. I was hoping we'd have intimate time when we arrived at my house, but Tony reluctantly explained that he was tired and needed to rest. We kissed good-bye, savoring our beautiful time together.

THIRTY-SIX

Passing the Test

*T*he next morning began with a message from Mary.

Hello, my sweet sister,

You are doing well, as you already know. You have gone through a difficult passage, a kind of test, which you passed. Because of that growth, you've come through a transition, as if through a birth canal into a new, stronger, more advanced level of spiritual beingness for you.

You are learning to stay the course with your consciousness in the midst of powerful emotions. This is like weathering a storm at sea. When your emotions arise powerfully, you often start to think in ways that are not accurate. Your dark side and fears take over. This is the storm of your mind.

In the passage that you just went through, you experienced powerful emotions of grief, loss, and shock over your separation from Tony, after five days of virtual unity with him. As you experienced these intense feelings and weren't able to come into intimacy with Tony in the way you had during your trip, you started to tell yourself that your relationship with him was over, your desires for energy-based intimacy were too much, you would never be able to have a successful relationship, you would always push men away, and so forth.

However, what you did this time period was different: You observed the thoughts you were having, and you held them with the awareness

213

that they may not be accurate because of the emotions you were feeling. You brought your consciousness, your Divine Masculine, to the circumstance, and allowed that part of yourself to be strong and to exercise discernment. This helped you weather the storm.

The storm was not bad or unnecessary. It was necessary, given your ability to handle your emotions. You eventually became conscious of the source of your emotions, which was the loss of your connection and closeness with Tony in an ongoing and continuous way. And you were able to talk with Tony about this, which allowed him to express that he was experiencing the same thing.

You correctly understood and expressed that your difficulty in connecting intimately was an indicator of feelings you weren't in touch with. Had you been conscious of this possibility in the moment, you could have chosen to stop trying to be intimate and instead explore together what emotions were affecting you that you were not aware of. Doing this in the future when such circumstances occur will help you bypass the suffering caused by the storm of your emotions and the concomitant thoughts that arise with it.

Eventually you will be able to traverse this with much greater ease, because you will do away with the stage of separating from the person you are experiencing the emotion with. You will explore the emotions together as they arise and allow them to do their work of bringing you to the inner divine qualities that need attending to. You then will be able to attend to those qualities together and make choices together about the actions or changes you wish to take.

All of this may require some time to manifest and may occur in stages or steps. That you have opened the doorway for this to take place represents more growth than you realize.

You may choose to do other supportive things in the midst of going through a dark emotional time, such as limiting aspects of your work that take away from your productivity; not using alcohol to avoid pain but only drinking as a form of celebration; and staying balanced through getting enough sleep, tending to your environment, and reaching out to friends. Most important, however, is the discipline you are learning to bring to your thoughts by holding the possibility that they may not be accurate, rather than believing them and being dragged through the emotional roller coaster doing so creates.

Regarding your engagement with your past partner, you have seen that this is not serving you, that you become emotionally imbalanced and disturbed when you interact with him. Many others have seen this and reported it to you, but you have not been ready to take responsibility for this. Your love for him has blinded you to the negative effect upon you of relating to him. And you have been waiting for him to change. Finally you are shifting in accurately seeing that your interactions with him are placing your relationship with Tony at risk, a correct observation that is now motivating you to end the energetic vampirism that has been occurring.

It takes strength for you to close that doorway to him because you like the energy rush that you get from your connection to him. You have confused this with love. But it has its price, as you have observed. You understand that you can still love him in a pure way but that you require boundaries, given the kind of energetic interactions you and he have. I support your growing in this way. Indeed, I feel it is essential for your emotional equilibrium and openheartedness.

All this is most positive, and I commend you for your work and growth. It has been necessary for you to do this work in order to continue on the path we have embarked upon. I support you and assure you that you are still fully engaged in this path and process with me.

In love and tender holding,
I AM Mary Magdalene

THIRTY-SEVEN

Reconnection

*T*ony came over around 5:30 Friday evening. I greeted him with a long kiss and his response was obvious. Other than seeing each other at dance class, we hadn't spent time together since the previous weekend. The last three days had been energetically intense, and I'd been longing to be close to Tony's body, wanting to feel his stabilizing, centering, grounding influence.

Almost immediately, we moved into the bedroom and soon were holding each other. Tony initiated a few sexual caresses, but I told him, "I'm not ready yet. I have emotions I need to talk about."

"Let's do the sharing process," he replied, which I greatly appreciated.

"I can begin," I said. "I've been feeling disconnected from you. At this stage of our relationship, it doesn't work for me to alternate between being so close and then having periods of not seeing each other or talking for many days. It's painful for me, and I end up shutting down and disconnecting.

"I've been realizing that I don't really know what is happening with you," I continued. "I don't know whether any of the things we've talked about are going to happen because we don't have any definite plans, nothing tangible. It all seems like dreams. I'm starting to think the only thing I really have is the present moment of our connecting. We don't have any real commitment beyond that."

Tony seemed to reel. He told me, "I feel like I've been kicked in the stomach." He started to leave, but I knew that would only lead to more separation between us.

"I would like you to stay so we can go through our pain together," I implored.

"Why?" he asked. "I'm already in pain. I don't like feeling this way."

"I see going through pain together as an opportunity for great intimacy between people," I replied. "It's engaging Mary's process of embracing pain, which she described in the first book, only doing it together as a couple, letting it lead you together to a new place of depth and connection."

Tony softened. "I've seen that going through pain together can be quite bonding," he allowed. "I'm willing to give it a try." I felt relieved and grateful to him for his trust in me and in Mary.

"Let's start by identifying the inner divine qualities we each are having," I suggested. Focusing on that brought a deeper level of calm to both of us.

"I'm needing connection—and continuity of our connection," I said.

"I want to be understood that I'm following through on what we've talked about," Tony stated. "I also need balance in handling all the different parts of my life. I'm feeling overwhelmed with all I'm trying to do."

That gave me an idea. "Is there someone you could hire to help you?" I asked.

That sparked a thought for him. "Actually, I've given a lot of help to Joanie over the past year. I'm sure I could call upon her for support." I sensed his energy lightening with this new inspiration, and he confirmed that he felt better.

Next we started to address his need for being understood. I said, "I don't hear much from you about what steps you're taking to follow through with things we've talked about. That makes it hard for me to understand what's going on."

"I intentionally don't talk about what's going on with me," he explained. "It's been challenging, and sometimes frustrating, to make the changes I want to make. I keep all that to myself as a way of not bringing the painful parts of my life to you."

"I appreciate your wanting to protect me," I affirmed. "But the result is I'm not feeling connected to a great deal of your world. I love you and want to be close to all the parts of you."

"I understand that now from this conversation," he replied. "I agree to share what is happening in the future with you."

The energy was starting to flow between us, and we both could feel it. But I still needed more completion. It seemed like we'd addressed Tony's needs for balance and understanding, and my needs for connection. The one that was still unresolved was my need for continuity in our connection. This seemed to be the tough one for us to talk about because the only solutions we could readily come up with, such as living together or getting married, seemed to require things that one or the other of us didn't want to do.

"I see this as an open-ended moment in which we can cocreate something new in our relationship," I suggested, "possibly something neither one of us has thought of before. I think we should say whatever comes to us, even if it seems impossible or crazy, because those thoughts may lead to other ideas. Or we might come up with ways to refine them that are doable." I was specifically thinking of the idea of living together, which I would have liked but Tony probably wouldn't, at least not at this time. I screwed up my courage and said, "One possibility is that we could live together." To my relief, Tony seemed to accept it as part of our brainstorming pool.

Then I suggested, "We could schedule times that we that we commit to spending together each week. That would give me something concrete to depend on. Maybe we could agree on several evenings and one weekend day." In saying that, I realized that the time of day we spend together made a huge difference for me. "You know, my energy is much stronger during the daytime than at night. So my sense of connection from spending time together during the day is much stronger. One daytime occasion of being together will carry me much further than several nighttime ones."

Now our energy was flowing even more and Tony began stroking my back. But I still wasn't ready to receive his caresses. I asked him, "Would you keep touching me, but with stillness instead of movement?" He complied but his energy waned. We then turned our focus to our seemingly opposite styles of responding to touch. "This is another challenge we seem to be having," I commented. "I love still touch and often find my energy blocked when I receive a lot of movement. You seem to be just the reverse—finding your connection through movement and losing it when you're still."

That led to another idea. "Let's try something we haven't explored before," I proposed. "Let's alternate turns of one person moving while the other one remains still." We tried it, and it felt good to both of us. Tony showed his enjoyment with a nibble on my nipple.

I immediately reacted with a lot of charge, saying, "I'm not ready for that!"

"OK," Tony replied and then seemed to withdraw his energy altogether. Suddenly I couldn't feel him at all. It was as though he had evaporated.

I felt overwhelmed with how difficult everything seemed between us and started to cry. I poured out a stream of feelings. "I don't want everything to be so hard. I don't want to feel like what feels good to me feels bad to you, or vice versa. I don't want to feel like I have to protect myself from your sexual advances, or that you're going to be sexual with me before I've opened up and am ready."

I had turned away from him, but Tony said, "Turn over and come back to me." He just held me. That felt really good. I didn't know what to do or where to go, and felt exhausted from trying.

I sensed a shift, and suddenly everything started to make sense. "It's only been a week and a half since we returned from our trip," I observed. "We felt so intimate and connected that whole time. I think I still haven't recovered from the shock of coming back to our usual routines and seeing so little of each other."

Tony agreed, saying, "It was a trauma to us and our relationship."

Finally we'd found the source of our disconnection. I could tell because our bodies and energy were magnetically drawn to each other again. We were back in sync and harmony. Without any more words, we undressed each other and slowly and lovingly moved into intimacy. I asked Tony to breathe into me, through his lingam and into my yoni. In the next breath, he was inside of me. We made exquisite love, with such depth and openness, remaining slow for most of the time and flowing naturally. Our love sounds were like music. And I particularly noticed a newfound ability to feel even more deeply into my yoni, which seemed to open me to a hidden chamber of even more pleasurable sensations.

Finally, we came to rest, both of us filled with love and beauty. We still felt our desire for each other but were able to rest in peace, holding each other close. Tony confided, "I've never experienced a process like we went through before." Then he added, "But I've never known anyone like you before."

"All us Sirians are like this!" I immediately quipped, humorously referring to beings from the star Sirius.

"Good for me to know," he replied, giving me a loving hug.

We held each other a long time, talking and enjoying the fullness of our connection once again. After a while, I playfully said, "I'm kicking you out because I have a full day ahead preparing for a presentation I'll be giving on Mary Magdalene."

We both began to get dressed. I got as far as putting my panties on when Tony looked at me with great appreciation. He came over to me on the bed, kissed me, and then slid my panties down and started pleasuring my yoni with his mouth. It was exquisite and he brought me to orgasm several times. At one point, I asked him to go slower. He became very slow, to which I responded with an emphatic "yes!" I orgasmed one more time. He came back to my mouth and gave me a huge kiss. Then he stood up and got dressed.

I had an hour and a half drive the next day for the presentation I was giving. Tony said, "I want you to call me when you arrive, call me when you leave to return home, and call again when you're close to home." We planned when we'd see each other again, and I felt very loved and cared for.

THIRTY-EIGHT

Depths of Merging

*T*he day after my presentation on Mary Magdalene, I reflected on the event. I had worn the crystal necklace Tony had given me, and many people had commented on how striking and powerful it was. When I asked for questions after the presentation, one woman said she was being guided to ask me about the pendant and what the connection was between Isis and the crystal. I was amused, as I felt her clearly picking up on the meaning and message of the necklace. I especially enjoyed telling people the piece was a gift from my beloved partner.

During the questions there were several requests for me to channel Mary. I asked Mary if she wanted to communicate with people, and she very graciously agreed, giving a beautiful message and answering questions people asked of her.

Today I was very tired. As usual, I wasn't aware of how much energy I'd expended while giving the presentation and channeling, until I felt the effects afterward.

Tony arrived in the evening. We enjoyed our time eating dinner together and sharing about our day, finishing with chai tea. Then we moved into the office and read aloud the recent communication from Mary. At a certain point, we shifted into talking about the sacred sexuality workshop I was going to lead the following weekend. I asked Tony, "Are you still open to leading the men's empowerment part of the evening ritual?"

"I'd be happy to do that," he replied. "Just let me know what you have in mind."

Before long it was 9:00 p.m. Tony said, "I'm tired. I think I should go."

"I feel disappointed," I said. "I wanted to have intimate time together."

Tony seemed surprised. "I didn't know that's what you were wanting. But I can stay." I felt happy that he was receptive to what I wanted and willing to stay longer.

We moved into the bedroom, which was quite chilly. The November weather had turned suddenly cold the past few days, and we could feel it inside. We turned the heater up and snuggled under my comforters. I told Tony, "I don't necessarily want to have sex. I just want to lie next to you and feel your body." He seemed comfortable with that.

We drew close, and I spoke again. "I've been reading a book about relationships and sexuality. The author suggests that couples share with each other what sexuality provides for them, being specific about the different activities and their effects. I was thinking I'd like to do that with you."

We both felt a little stumped about how to describe our experiences. "Why don't we start with kissing," I suggested. We kissed and then shared what we experienced while kissing.

Tony went first. "Kissing provides connection with my heart."

"When we kiss," I said, "I can feel my sexual energy moving outward from my heart, first into my breasts and then down my spine to my genitals."

We kept kissing. At one point Tony added, "Sexuality provides stability and balance. I'm surprised about the stability part, but that's what's coming to me."

"Sexuality opens me up," I revealed. "It makes me feel soft and feminine and beautiful. I also love the feeling of giving myself to your manliness." All of a sudden we noticed we were super warm, and we both had a simultaneous urge to take off our clothes. We removed our clothing and then embraced again.

I moved so that the tip of Tony's lingam was just touching my pearl (our name for my clitoris). I felt extremely turned on and said, "I love to feel you right there." We began moving ever so slightly and were both extremely excited. Tony slowly ran his hand over my bottom and touched my yoni ever so lightly. I shrieked with joy. I pulled him on top of me and softly said, "Breathe through your lingam into my yoni." He slid inside me, and we were in bliss. He kept breathing into me again and again, moving into a new depth of merging. My mind dissolved as we rode a wave of ecstasy over and over again.

We came to rest and held each other. I handed Tony the lubricant, and he knew just what I was wanting. He squeezed it into his hand and then lovingly spread the cool gel all over my yoni, which felt delicious. Next, I took it and spread it all over his lingam. We began making love again, this time in an ocean of lubrication and delight.

After resting again, I whispered to Tony, "I'd like you to enter me from behind." He was happy to do so, and soon we dissolved again in exquisite lovemaking.

THIRTY-NINE

Sharing with Others

*T*he following week was hectic because I was not only preparing for the upcoming sacred sexuality workshop but also being interviewed for a radio show and meeting a deadline for a magazine article. As if that weren't enough, on Tuesday I strained my back while moving a box of books and suddenly I was down for the count, in great pain.

I'd been through this before. It had started with a car accident five years earlier, resulting in periodic bouts of my back "going out" ever since, during which I would mostly lie in bed and rest, often for a week or more. The previous episode had occurred just before the International New Age Trade Show in Denver several months before, which I figured was due to stress.

Perhaps this episode was from stress, too, I told myself, thinking of all the preparations I was handling for the sacred sexuality workshop. For the remainder of the day I rested, punctuated with ice pack applications every hour that felt surprisingly good. Tony did a long-distance healing for me that night and then came over in the morning for a hands-on healing session. By Wednesday night, I was feeling tentatively hopeful that I would be able to lead the workshop the coming weekend. The next day I was better—and amazed at how quickly I was healing. That morning I saw the chiropractor, who confirmed that he thought I'd be OK for the workshop as long as I listened to my body and rested in the event of pain.

Tony came over on Friday, and we reviewed some of the movements I demonstrated in workshops so he could do them if I couldn't. By the end of our practice together, we were both turned on and we transitioned into making love, taking care to be gentle so as to avoid hurting my back. It felt good to reconnect intimately before the sacred sexuality workshop.

The workshop was small, which I appreciated since I felt physically weak from my back strain. It was also the first sacred sexuality workshop Tony had ever attended and the first one I'd led in six years. Tony was wearing several hats—assisting me, representing the man's point of view, and experiencing the material in a workshop setting, all for the first time. He was a natural in all his roles and the participants really appreciated his contributions.

On the first afternoon of the workshop, he struggled with tiredness, having pushed himself hard with construction work all week. However, by the time we began the evening's activities, he was fully energized and present. He led the empowerment process with the men while the women got dressed in their Goddess attire. The men's portion ended with them chanting to the women, calling us to come join them. We came in dancing and encircling them, filling them with our Divine Feminine energy. The energy kept building as I guided the group through a Shiva-Shakti ritual, exchanging energy through dancing for each other.[1] We ended ecstatically dancing with our partners. From there, we moved into a sensual feast, taking turns feeding our partners delicious and varied finger food, which they received with their eyes closed. By the end of the evening, the entire group had melted into a pool of pleasure.

The following day was even more fulfilling, especially in the afternoon when we all experienced an extended Tantric energy exchange with a partner. I could feel the fire of passion ignite between Tony and me, and he acknowledged it, too. I loved that we could feel so comfortable allowing our passion in front of others. We concluded with Tony and me demonstrating Tantric lovemaking positions with our clothes on and explaining how to bring the techniques everyone had learned into sexual intimacy. We were all soaring by the end and felt like we'd become friends for life.

Still high as we returned home, I asked Tony, "Would you like to spend some time together?"

"No. I'm tired and need to rest," he replied.

I was disappointed but understood it had been a big weekend for him. I went home and unpacked the car. It took about an hour for my adrenaline rush from teaching to dissipate, and then I crashed, too. Happily, it was a soft crash, cushioned by the sweetness of the group's appreciation and joy.

FORTY

Changing Course

The Monday after a workshop had always been null and void for me. This one was no different.

I was still tired on Tuesday, but my stepmom urged me to come to Albuquerque to visit my dad in his new home, a large hacienda-style house that had been converted into an assisted-living facility. I felt some trepidation, anticipating that he might be unhappy with the other residents in various end-of-life stages. To my delight, we found him sitting up in his wheelchair in the living room, looking alert and happy. Nearby, people were watching TV, which was the closest social interaction with other residents I'd seen him have in recent times.

Margaret led me to his bedroom and said, "I was wondering if you and Tony would hang some pictures and help turn your dad's room into a home. Maybe you could do that when you come on Thursday for Thanksgiving." I happily agreed.

Before we left, my dad introduced us to Stephen, an elderly resident he'd made friends with. "We're both veterans," my dad said proudly. "Stephen was in World War II . . . and the Korean War . . . and the Vietnam War."

"I don't think he was in Vietnam, Dad," I said gently, but my dad didn't believe me. I let it go, giving him a hug and kiss good-bye.

I returned to Santa Fe in time for my tango lesson and was disappointed not to find Tony at the studio. I guessed that he was losing interest in learning tango. He came over the next day so I could give him some hardware that needed replacing from my dad's dresser, and he explained why he'd missed dance class the night before. He said he'd been working hard over the past month helping his ex-wife find a new apartment to move into. She'd been set up to sign the lease the previous day, but at the last minute her friend who was to be the cosigner refused to show up, saying she didn't think it was a good situation. They lost the apartment, including the deposit Tony had put down and the hopes he'd been holding onto for gaining independence from his difficult situation. At that point, he was too deflated to go out dancing. I could see the exhausted look in his eyes and shoulders, and felt sad for him.

The next day was Thanksgiving. As we drove to Albuquerque, I caught myself sounding strident with Tony, which disturbed me. *What's going on with me?* I asked myself, then decided to put the dilemma aside and make the day as happy as I could for myself and everyone else.

We picked up a Thanksgiving meal for my dad, along with a light lunch for Margaret and us since we were attending another gathering later that afternoon. We then all met at my dad's home to enjoy Thanksgiving lunch together, after which Tony and I decorated my dad's room under his supervision. My dad, pleased with the results, even invited his new friend, Stephen, in to see his spruced- up room. I left feeling hopeful about my dad finally being well attended to in a place that felt like home.

After enjoying our Thanksgiving dinner with friends, we arrived back in Santa Fe at 10:00 p.m. and, exhausted, agreed to spend the next evening together. Once alone, I felt the disturbing energy I'd tucked aside earlier in the day come back to haunt me as my mind filled with disquieting thoughts. *Has Tony lost interest in me?* I wondered. *He seems to be working longer hours than ever and, at the end of the day, is too tired to do anything but eat and sleep. More importantly, have I lost interest in him?* Remembering the love and devotion with which the men at the sacred sexuality workshop had looked at their partners, I realized that I, too, wanted to be looked at that way. *Perhaps it's time to open to dating again,* I thought.

I woke up the next morning feeling heavy hearted, sensing that I was starting to let go of my relationship with Tony. He called an hour later to talk about our plans for the evening and asked how I was. Impulsively I blurted out, "I'm really sad. Lots of feelings are coming up about our relationship, and I just feel dejected about what's happening with us."

"What would you like to do?" Tony asked.

"I would like to talk," I said. We agreed to get together after lunch.

Tony arrived an hour and a half later than when we'd agreed on. As we sat down, I said, "I'm not happy in our relationship . . ."

To my surprise, Tony jumped in with his own communication: "I've come to realize that I've been working so much to avoid dealing with my ex-wife and all her problems. I need to address that situation and devote my energies to extricating myself from her life. I want to get her set up so her needs are provided for and I'm not responsible for helping her anymore. In order to make that happen, I've decided to stop working and just focus on what I need to handle with her. I've also decided I can't continue to be with you. I need to just complete with my ex-wife and become free."

I felt myself coming to peace, the way I always did when the truth was finally spoken. "I feel happy for you," I said, and I meant it. "I think you're doing what you really need to be doing and what's going to support you the most. I'm also sad because I feel my loss."

He seemed relieved to be receiving my support and understanding.

We spoke more, hugging and holding each other several times. After a while, Tony said, "I love you, and I appreciate all that you've brought into my life."

"I love you, too," I replied, "and I want the best for you." Then we said good-bye, and he left.

As the day went on, I felt a strange combination of relief, peace, disorientation, and numbness. In the evening I talked to a close friend on the phone, telling her what had transpired. She questioned whether we were addressing the real issue. "Did something come up for Tony at the sacred sexuality workshop?" she asked.

I thought back to the sharing exercises we had done the previous weekend around the question "What is one of your sexual fears?" Tony had said he had a fear of losing his sexual energy if he slowed down to the unhurried pace I enjoyed while first connecting. I now wondered if addressing that challenge was just one too many difficulties for Tony to take on amidst so much else.

FORTY-ONE

Speed of Light

*T*hat night I couldn't sleep. At 4:00 a.m., my body was missing Tony terribly and my mind was filled with questions: *If Tony stops working and spends his time bringing his affairs with his ex-wife to closure, couldn't he still see me in the evenings? Is this really about him being disturbed by our sexual differences around pacing? Have I been too demanding? Could I be more supportive of him and give him energy for the ordeal he's going through?*

I decided to text him to see if we could work things out. I wrote to him: "I'm up and thinking about us."

He immediately texted back: "I'm up, too."

"Do you want to come over?" I asked, but I didn't receive a response. Feeling discouraged, I decided to try again and wrote: "I would like to get together to talk. What do you think about that?"

After a few minutes, I saw a new text waiting to be opened. Tony had responded: "I'll see you in a while. I'll text you when I get there." I felt relief, excitement, and hope, all mixed together.

Before I knew it, he was at the door. I took his hat and coat, and we moved into my office. The moment we faced each other, we were drawn together like two magnets. It was hard not to melt into each other, but I wanted to share my thoughts and feelings so they wouldn't submerge into blocks between us. I told Tony I wanted to do that and asked, "Would you like to lie down on the bed to talk?"

"I'd love to," he said.

When we stepped into the bedroom, Tony immediately began removing his clothes. I felt a little more cautious, just taking off my slippers and socks. We held each other close, and I poured out all that I was thinking, including what I thought might be going on regarding our sexuality.

"I think you're right," he agreed. "I think the challenge of matching your pacing was overwhelming me but I hadn't realized it. I'm also seeing that separating doesn't solve things—talking about them does. When we talk, our energy opens up and we feel our attraction to each other stronger than ever. Then we make love and feel super-connected again."

"I want to commit to doing that, as best we can," I said.

"Me, too," Tony said with a smile. Then he pointed out, "This was our shortest breakup so far."

I joked, "Maybe our breakups will get faster and faster till they're the speed of light—before we even have time to think about breaking up, we'll already be through it!"

We laughed and were filled with such passion we could hardly get my clothes off fast enough. Then I pulled Tony on top of me and asked, "Will you breathe through your lingam into me?" He tenderly complied and entered me. I was filled with a wave of intense joy and pleasure as I received him, immediately followed by my bursting out in sobs, saying, "I don't want you to leave."

Tony held me and replied, "I'm here with you now."

"I can feel that," I said, "but I still have sadness, and now fear, too. I'm afraid to open again."

"Yes, you have sadness and fear," Tony acknowledged, continuing to hold me. Once recognized and shared, it dissolved away.

We made exquisite love for a very long time, expressing how deeply we love and value each other. Eventually we came to rest, concerned about my being sore afterward. However, we felt so much sexual energy, we continued moving the energy up and down our spines and having orgasms, even though we were lying next to each other. Finally, I turned over and we made love again for another extended period until at last we felt complete.

I reflected on the Tantric understanding of a woman's Goddess spot, or G-spot, as the place where she holds sexual trauma.[1] I asked Tony, "Would you do some healing work on my Goddess spot to help relieve my yoni soreness?" Even though the prior healings seemed real and effective, I still wasn't entirely free of the painful symptoms.

"I'd be happy to," he replied. "I don't want you to be sore."

"Me either," I agreed. "And I want to be free to make love as frequently as we wish in the future."

Tony began by lovingly spreading cool gel over my yoni, outside and in. Then he began his healing. I was amazed how he immediately went to all the spots where I was sore. I could feel the soreness go away with his touch. A few spots were very pleasurable. I especially felt the pleasure moving from my third eye up to my crown.

To support and celebrate his healing work, I'd recently bought Tony a gift for his birthday, which was a little over a month away. It was a special crystal that had been infused with healing energy. Excited about giving it to him, I jokingly said, "We should at least stay together till your birthday because I already have your present," Being together felt so simple and free.

Tony told me, "All afternoon I was thinking about what

we've been doing with following Mary's instruction. I felt disturbed about discontinuing before we'd completed the whole process." He stated emphatically, "We started it together and we should finish it together."

Maybe it will never be finished, I thought.

FORTY-TWO

Partner Ankh

When Tony called the next night, I surprised him by saying, "I'd like to ask you out on a date for tomorrow evening."

"What kind of date?" he asked

"A lovemaking date," I told him. "I want to engage the partner ankh practice Mary gave about a month ago." Although we had tried this once while resting and holding each other, we hadn't yet included it during our lovemaking.

Tony responded enthusiastically, "Yes, that sounds wonderful."

He arrived promptly at 5:00 p.m. We kissed passionately, both obviously ready for our tryst. We started by reviewing Mary's instructions for the ankh practice, beginning with the solo ankh breathing practice (see figure 25-1) and moving on to the partner ankh practice (see figure 33-2). After reading each one, we practiced it energetically, sitting in the chairs in my office with our clothes on. We went through the breathing and movements while directing our energy along the various circuits. It felt very strong. By the time we finished, we were both blissed out. We could have stopped there and been very satisfied. In fact, Tony seemed to have forgotten that we were going to make love. But I remembered.

I took Tony's hand and led him to the bedroom, turning on my favorite lovemaking music. It was a little chilly in the room, so we both took off everything except our underwear and got close under the covers. I like to keep my panties on, and sometimes my bra, too, until I'm aroused. It creates a sense of safety, making me feel that I won't be touched in more vulnerable places until I'm ready. That helps me relax and ultimately open up. The understanding between Tony and me was that until those items of clothing were removed, I didn't want to be touched there. Tony, having learned my preferences, lovingly accommodated me.

As we held each other, I could feel the charged sexual energy flowing between us. We began kissing and stroking, with little moans escaping from my throat. Tony's hand flowed down my back and he slipped one of his fingers under the top of my panties. Caught off guard, I immediately froze, like a deer in headlights.

I told Tony, "I got afraid just now when you touched me under my panties."

I felt him tensing and pulling back his energy, so I asked, "What's going on?"

"I feel cautious," he answered, "like I've done something wrong."

I recognized the familiar dynamic that had typically led us to getting stuck. But this time was different. I was still feeling blissful from the partner ankh practice and found it uncharacteristically easy to keep my energy light and happy.

"I think we're having the same experience," I said. "We're both feeling afraid, and we've both withdrawn our energy."

"Would you hold me and stroke me?" Tony requested.

Touched by his vulnerability, I was happy to do so, though I still didn't feel our energies connecting. "How about if I spread coconut oil over your lingam?" I asked Tony.

"That sounds great," he replied.

I began by slowly removing his underwear. Then I dipped my fingers in the oil and, deliberately and lovingly, spread it over him. I began at the tip of his lingam, swirled around to under the head, and slowly moved down the shaft to the base. My libations felt beautiful and sacred, as well as arousing, reminding me of devotional worship in the Indian tradition, where a holy object is anointed with oil.

"I feel like I'm anointing you," I murmured.

He responded, saying, "You are."

I removed my remaining clothes and drew him to me. Together we breathed him inside of me. We began making love, but soon I paused, saying, "I don't feel our energies connected at the heart, and I don't want to make love without that."

"Do you want me to come out?" Tony asked.

"No, I like having you inside me." Sensing that we were trying too hard, I suggested, "Let's just be still for a bit." We relaxed into quietness. Within seconds, an enormous swell of desire moved between us and seemed to pick both of us up. Our bodies knew just what to do—instantly we were passionately making love.

While still enjoying the natural expression of our sexual fire, I said, "I'd like to try the partner ankh practice." We shifted into breathing and moving synchronously, then began the Tantric wave, moving our sexual energy up to our crowns and down to our genitals. We alternated this with the partner ankh: breathing up to our hearts, looping the energy out the back of our hearts, over our heads, down each other's back, and entering each other's heart from the back. We completed the energy circuit by breathing our energy down each other's three lower chakras, finally meeting and blending our energies at our genitals.

Moving our energies in this pattern gave a deeper sense of merging than we'd experienced before. It immediately led to a powerful orgasm, where I saw a brilliant internal light in the space between my third eye and crown. Tony later confirmed that he saw the same light.

We repeated the pattern again, now alternating the Tantric wave with the partner ankh several times before exploding in deep waves of orgasm and light. Our lovemaking continued in a dance of our own creation, freely integrating the energy pathways, movements, and breathing with our spontaneous desires and initiations. It was glorious, a new experience of rapture for both of us.

We came to rest holding each other close, each filled with a vibration of ecstasy throughout our whole being. I couldn't stop my body from undulating with pleasure, and soon we were making love again, this time in the scissors position. When we stopped, it was only because we wanted to keep my yoni from being sore the next day.

I asked Tony, "Would you put some gel on my yoni for extra healing?"

He immediately shifted into his healer mode, tending to me with great care. His touch was exceedingly pleasurable, and soon I erupted in yet another extended orgasm. My desire to have Tony inside me rose up again, and he entered me for a bit more sweet, deep-hearted loving.

As we embraced, Tony said, "I'm so grateful to Mary for all she's giving us. And I thank you for being so receptive to me." That really touched my heart, reassuring me that Tony experiences me as receptive even as I find my voice and increasingly express what I would like in our sexuality.

Then we both felt another appetite arising—this time for food since we hadn't had dinner.

As we got dressed, Tony told me an amusing story: "Lately I've been feeling other people's sexual energy. Earlier today, while doing repairs in a couple's home I could feel, at a certain point, that the man was turned on and had an erection. I saw him whisper something to his wife, who then turned to me and said, 'I'll be out in my studio.' She immediately left, with her husband following quickly on her heels. They were gone about forty-five minutes. When they returned, the husband seemed uncomfortable being around me, but the wife, who appeared happy, engaged me in conversation.

I asked Tony, "Is sensing other people's sexual energy something new for you?"

"Yes, it is," he replied.

"Do you get turned on when you feel their arousal?" I inquired.

"I do, a little," he confided. I felt happy for him. I also wondered what it might be like for him to be in a space with a lot of people. Would he feel everyone's sexual energy?

That night, as I was going to sleep, I felt a vortex of energy from my yoni to my heart. I was still vibrating with the pleasure of our lovemaking, still feeling Tony inside of me, until I drifted off into a luxurious sleep.

I awoke the next morning to this text from him:

Good morning sweetie,

How are you feeling this morning? I woke up thinking of our loving yesterday afternoon. It was exquisite and over the top. Have a magical and joyful day, filled with my love.

xxx

PART III

Advanced Practices

FORTY-THREE

Goalless Exploration

*T*wo days later I received this message from Mary.

Greetings, my beloved sister,

It has been a while since we have connected in this way. I am happy to be communicating with you again.

You have done very well engaging the practices I have given you thus far. The last one you did, the partner ankh practice, was highly significant and marked a completion of the intermediate phase for you and Tony. The mastery you have both accomplished may not seem like work, as it was done in the midst of love and pleasure. But indeed, it required a degree of discipline and commitment, which you have both remained devoted to. For that I acknowledge you.

Once someone experiences the bliss these practices generate, the discipline and commitment becomes more attractive. For some, the engagement of these practices is a profound part of their spiritual life. This is because the practices reconnect them with higher states that they both long for and, at a soul level, remember. Some individuals are initially drawn to practice sacred sexuality because of the greater pleasure and heart connection they experience through this body of work, which then becomes a doorway to higher states of consciousness and being. Others, who more directly connect with the higher states, immediately recognize sacred sexuality as a valuable pathway for experiencing them.

Ultimately, sacred sexuality goes beyond the experiences you have. It is part of the transformational process of a whole life devoted to spiritual growth. This body of work is specifically transformative for the etheric (energy) body and for opening the heart. It is also aligned to and supportive of practices that work with consciousness and opening the higher mind. The more an individual has raised their level of consciousness, the easier the sacred sexuality practices will be. Similarly, the more sensitive and attuned an individual has become to their own and others' energy, the easier these practices will be. Whatever one's level of mastery, these practices are an avenue for strengthening one's attunement to energy and one's ability to access higher levels of consciousness.

Now you and Tony are ready to begin the advanced level of practices, which involve two primary directions. One is to work with raising the life-force energy in the spine, which, as you know, is called sekhem in the Egyptian tradition and kundalini in the Indian tradition. The other focus entails allowing yourself to be carried, primarily through stillness, into altered states of consciousness. We will work with both, as they each approach the transformation of your energy body and consciousness in a different way.

You actually began incorporating stillness in your last time of lovemaking. This opened you to a powerful force of energy that carried you to a higher level of connection and flow. Your next step is to simply play with periods of stillness in your lovemaking and see what you experience. You can do this even before you are in physical union, as you begin to connect through touch. Allow yourself to move into spaces of stillness—breathing, relaxing, and feeling—as you rest in the non-movement. Observe your energy, and see what happens.

Greater trust may now be required, for you are releasing the physical and moving into a purely energetic exchange. It may help to view this as an experiment, with no goal in mind, simply to see what happens. Do not be concerned if you lose your sense of connection or sexual arousal. Let that be part of the exploration and see what happens when that occurs.

I love you and bless you in your continued work and growth.
I AM Mary Magdalene

FORTY-FOUR

Returning to Center

After a busy weekend of a book fair, a presentation, and leading a workshop, I was happy to accept Tony's invitation to get together for a relaxing evening. As usual, we moved into lovemaking, but it was much shorter than usual and, for me, a bit hollow. I woke up the next morning with my yoni feeling sore. I was sure the discomfort was connected to my ambivalence about making love the night before, as I hadn't really been true to myself and my values. I needed to find my voice again, which I seemed to have lost in my relating with Tony. My phone wasn't working, so I sent Tony an email:

> Good morning, sweetie,
>
> My yoni is very sore this morning, and I'm having a challenging time. Please send me healing energy.
>
> I'm thinking I need to support my yoni by doing things differently in our lovemaking. Here's what's coming up for me.
>
> It's really important for me to wait until my yoni is fully open and lubricated before I have you enter inside me. Sometimes I rush into making love too soon. If we breathe together and take more time before making love, I think I will be better able to feel when I'm ready.
>
> Then I want to continue breathing together in the midst of

our lovemaking. I especially like to do this as we engage the Tantric wave or the partner ankh. And I want to connect with our hearts in the breathing and the movement.

I also think I need to move more slowly in our lovemaking—not 100 percent slower, but in a range between slow and medium, with some stillness interspersed.

This probably sounds like a lot, but really I see it as a transition to making love in a fully Tantric way. This isn't easy for me because it takes a level of discipline (Masculine energy) I don't naturally want to engage when I'm turned on and involved sexually. I just want to be in my Feminine side of surrendering, opening, and flowing with my desire. But I think this is what my body is calling me to do. I think my yoni soreness is supporting me to make this shift.

I want to ask for your help in making these changes. It would mean a lot to me if I knew you were committed to doing this with me. Together I think we can make this shift.

What do you think?

Much love,

Mercedes

I didn't hear back from Tony for several hours, so I re-sent the email. He wrote back: "I didn't see the email, but I'll look at it. Don't forget about choir rehearsal this evening. Do you want to go together?" I liked that idea.

As we drove to the rehearsal that night, I asked him about the email. He said, "I only read it quickly and don't really remember all of what you said. I did feel that you weren't ready for me last night when I entered you. It's uncomfortable for me, too, when that happens." I hadn't realized that he was also negatively affected by entering me prematurely. We both agreed to wait till I was all-the-way ready in the future.

Before he dropped me off at home that night, he mentioned he'd be coming over early in the morning to repair the kitchen fan for my housemate. "I think you should come over really early," I said, half in jest, "like around five." He liked that idea, and so did I.

I felt excited as I got ready for bed, putting on a pretty nightgown for him and leaving my phone by the bed. I woke up several times in the early morning eager to see him and finally got up around 7:30 a.m. to start my day.

When Tony arrived at 10:30 a.m. to do the repair, I asked him, "What happened this morning?"

"I didn't wake up till eight, and then I got busy," he told me.

"I understand if you overslept," I said, "but why didn't you call after you woke up to let me know? When you say you're going to do something and then don't do it, I feel like I don't matter." I could hear myself replaying a previous conversation as if reiterating a script that no longer had life to it.

"I'm sorry. You do matter," he replied, and then quickly started to work on the repair.

I felt horrible. Something was terribly off. I went into my office but couldn't concentrate on a thing. When Tony finished the repair, he came into my office and reminded me that we were having dinner with his friend Joanie the following night. Then he left.

I was engulfed with confusion and upset. *What's going on? Why didn't he come over earlier or call?* I asked myself.

I tried to get some work done but couldn't focus. I felt like I was in a dream, walking through the motions of being productive, trying to function mechanically. But my mind was gone and my heart was hurting. Finally in the midafternoon, I went to my altar and meditated. At last I came to peace.

Breathing into my belly, I relaxed into acceptance of the present circumstances, allowing my own integration to emerge. I told myself,

I don't understand what's happening with Tony. Maybe my email pushed him over the edge. Maybe he doesn't want to continue following Mary's instructions. Maybe the advanced practices seems too daunting or threatening. Maybe he doesn't feel the same level of desire for me that I feel for him. Figuring there was some degree of truth to all those ideas, I moved into deeper acceptance. With that came peace.

Feeling clear again, I affirmed to myself, *I know what's important to me, but I'm not in charge of Tony's choices or his heart. I love him—yet if we're not meant to be in relationship, I can accept that. What I have choice about is my spiritual work. It's doing that that feeds my heart the most.*

Gratitude welled up within me as I returned to my spiritual center and to peace.

I went to my dance classes that evening, first the intermediate tango and then the advanced studio class, which focused on a different dance form each week. Tony had long since stopped coming to his beginning tango class. I shared with several friends that I'd had a rotten day. Nonetheless dancing, as always, returned me to my joy. I particularly enjoyed how the teacher of the advanced class pushed me beyond my limits. It was exhilarating to feel my muscles come to life, doing more than I realized I could. I really felt like I was dancing and beautiful.

After the second class, my friend Chuck said he was going to a blues dance at a nearby club and asked if I'd like to join him. I'd gone dancing with him and his group of friends a few times in the past, and it had always been great fun. So I readily accepted, thinking this could be just what I needed to get out of my slump.

We arrived in time to get a table. Chuck started dancing with me before the music began, whirling me around the floor with the tango moves we were learning. I loved how free he was. Then the musicians began playing, and we switched gears into get-down blues, with lots of fun improvisation. After many dances, Chuck and I sat down at our table and began opening up about our personal lives. He shared a painful experience he'd gone through with his son the previous week. He also talked about the growth work he'd been doing in his relationship with his wife. He then asked me, "Do you want to talk about why you had such a rotten day today?"

I hoped that speaking about what was going on, especially with a man, would help me. I started by describing the big picture of recent events with Tony, since this was the first time I'd ever opened up about our relationship.

Chuck seemed to "get it" very quickly, affirming that my conclusions and guesses were well founded. "I can tell you've been thinking about this a lot," he observed. "You seem to have a good understanding of what's going on and why." He then said, very candidly, "Now you have a choice to make."

I felt the truth of what he was saying. Somehow, hearing about my situation from a man who had no investment in my decision as he looked me in the eye and told me what he thought, affected me deeply. I felt another dose of Masculine energy and power as he followed up with, "You probably already know the outcome."

"The best outcome I could imagine," I replied, "would be for Tony to choose to have the kind of relationship with me that I want to have with him, which means being married." I then said, "My guess is the only way that would happen would be for us to separate and for him to figure out on his own that that's his desire. But I'm not sure he wants to be in a relationship right now or, if he does, that I'm the one he would choose. More likely, we'll separate and one or both of us will move on to another relationship. Actually, I suspect Tony wants the benefits of a relationship, but not a relationship."

Chuck acknowledged the validity of my conclusions. He then said, "Now you have to go through the difficult steps of grieving the loss—denial, anger, bargaining, depression, and acceptance."

"I'm aware of that," I concurred. "I think I've been experiencing those stages in increments all along, in response to not having the closeness I've wanted with Tony. So separating from him may not be as hard to go through as it otherwise would."

As I left, I felt grateful—for dancing, for friends, for men who shared their Masculine strength with me even when they weren't my partner, and for Spirit's willingness to provide for me even when my world seemed to be falling apart.

I came home and put clean sheets on my bed, preparing to begin a new chapter of my life.

FORTY-FIVE

Grief

The next evening, I split up with Tony. I'd asked him to talk, but for days it seemed he'd been avoiding my efforts at conversation, probably knowing what I was going to say.

We had dinner with Joanie, as planned. I arrived before Tony and told her what was going on, woman to woman. I said, "I could use a drink," and she opened a bottle of wine. Tony arrived just as we were filling the glasses. Emboldened by the wine and Joanie's support, I asked Tony as we were leaving, "Would you be willing to talk with me?" He said he was, and we agreed to meet at my house to talk.

Parting turned out to be very simple. "I want to end our relationship," I told him. "I've been feeling things were off for a couple of weeks, but the incident a few days ago—with you not coming over and not calling—really put me over the edge. I don't like the way I'm being treated."

"I've been feeling the same thing about ending our relationship," Tony replied. "I feel overwhelmed with my life, and I have no excess to give to you. It's really not about you at all."

"I think that's the problem," I said. I knew he was being honest and didn't mean to hurt me with his last statement, but it was painful to hear nonetheless. I wanted it to be about me!

Tony said, "I want you to know how grateful I am for our relationship and for all I've experienced with you." Then he started for the door.

I stopped him, saying, "Wait. I don't feel complete. I want us to express what we're feeling to each other." Tony looked surprised but was willing. I took a breath and began. "I feel sad—about a lot of things." I started to cry. "More than anything I'm sad about the dreams I had for the two of us. I feel the loss of my dreams. I'm sad we won't be creating a life together, growing old together, teaching workshops together, taking trips together, creating a home and a retreat center together. I'm sad about being alone.

"I'm afraid, too. I'm afraid of not ever having the kind of relationship I want. I'm afraid I'm not attractive enough or that I push men away. I'm worried about how I'm going to fulfill Mary's instruction without you. And I'm going to miss seeing your grandchildren, whom I've become very fond of."

Then Tony spoke. "I'm sad, too," he said. "I'm sad about not completing the work we've been engaging with Mary. I've valued Mary's teachings so much and all I've learned from them. I don't want to be alone, either. You've brought me back to life from a long time of being alone. I'll miss all the fun we have together and traveling together. I'll miss feeling loved by you. And I'll miss our lovemaking."

Then we fell silent. I knew there was more I wanted to say. I wanted to tell Tony all the things I was grateful for in our relationship, but I wasn't ready yet. Expressing gratitude would have taken me away from experiencing my feelings of grief and loss and into my head, trying to do the "right" thing rather than the real thing. I told him, "I want to express my gratitude to you another time, when it's real for me."

He understood and accepted my sentiments. Collecting the few things he had at my house, we said good-bye with a hug and a kiss. Then he left.

I felt proud of us for separating with openness, honesty, and closeness. I felt peaceful and tired as well. Without much ado, I took myself to bed.

FORTY-SIX

New Beginnings

I felt surprisingly balanced the next day. I meditated; wrote a blog post about what might happen on December 21, which was now only two weeks away; sent out my newsletter; and headed to Albuquerque. There I stopped in at bookstores, including one that was hosting me for a book study group, and then visited my dad.

I found him in the living room of his new home, taking a nap in his wheelchair. He woke up in good spirits the moment I said "hello." During our time together I noticed him having more interactions with the other residents and greater ease in moving around the house and changing positions in his wheelchair. He cracked some really funny jokes, read a bit of the newspaper out loud to me, and told me about the beautiful Christmas music they'd listened to that morning—all signs that he was partaking in life and developing more abilities. Wanting me to watch him stand up on his own, he held on to the sink and pulled himself up, then grinned and waved as I took a picture of him with my cell phone. Mostly I saw that he was happy. And that made me very happy.

"Dad, I'm thinking we could set up your electric train around the Christmas tree in the living room here," I told him. "Would you like to do that?"

"Well, I wouldn't want to disturb the other residents or the dogs," he said, sounding worried.

"I think they'd enjoy having it here," I reassured him.

"Then I'd like that very much," he said with a twinkle in his eye.

On my drive back to Santa Fe, I reflected on how my father seemed to be "coming back" as the dad I'd always known at the very time I was letting go of Tony. That didn't strike me as mere coincidence. My father's most recent brush with death had begun almost immediately after Mary started communicating with me, and seemed to be concluding at the same time Tony and I were completing our work with her. Tony and my dad, the two primary males in my life, had both drawn me into experiences of the next dimension—my dad through his proximity with death and Tony through the ecstasy of sexuality. I couldn't help but think this was intentional, part of the grand plan of Spirit. Although sexuality and death are not generally considered analogous, at the moment I was seeing them both as avenues for accessing realms beyond our ordinary reality.

My thoughts shifted to Tony. I called and left him a message, saying, "I want to thank you for our conversation last night and all we shared. Even though we were parting, it felt really loving."

By the time Tony returned my call, I was back home. We had a warm, friendly conversation. He said how much he appreciated my latest blog, which meant a lot to me. I told him about my visit with my dad, including the plan to set up his train.

"If you'd like, I can go with you to help set it up," Tony offered. I felt a huge sense of relief and immediately accepted, knowing how mechanical he was.

I enjoyed our exchange, yet it felt odd to have such an open-hearted conversation with him and then say good-bye and let go.

FORTY-SEVEN

Doorway

*I*t was 12/12/12, which I considered a doorway leading to 12/21/12. For years I'd been hearing about December 21, 2012, as a day that would initiate great change. I had a feeling of excitement, sensing that something special was afoot. It reminded me of being young and looking forward to my birthday. Or being pregnant and awaiting the due date. I truly hoped it would be a birth day— for all of humanity—into a higher level of consciousness and spiritual awakening.

I felt light and buoyant, as though being lifted by an enormous energy. At 11:00 a.m., I participated in a global meditation that was synchronized with a group of people in Arkansas, peaking at 12:12 p.m. Arkansas time (11:12 a.m. my time). The focus for the meditation was peace, harmony, love, and the highest good for humanity, all kingdoms and realms of the Earth, and the entire cosmos in welcoming the new Earth.

At 12:12 p.m. Mountain Time, I was in the midst of a radio interview about my experiences with Mary Magdalene. I regarded this synchronicity as symbolic of the change I was going through, in which my spirituality was becoming less inward and less formal. Instead of being primarily expressed through meditation or ceremony, it was increasingly integrated with my actions in service to others and the world. My inner expressions of spirituality now seemed to continue on their own, without requiring the same kind of dedicated time and "work" as before.

Throughout the interview I felt carried by the energy of the day and especially sensed a powerful opening to the Divine Feminine. I imagined dancing in the streets with many women.

I had another interview later in the afternoon, which also felt very high energy. The interviewer was a devoted Christian, which made me wonder how Mary's messages would be received, by both the interviewer and her audience, as some of Mary's statements could have appeared challenging to those with conventional Christian views. Wanting to be sensitive to the beliefs of the host and her audience without compromising Mary's message, I asked Mary's guidance.

As it turned out, Mary's characteristic mix of compassion and revolutionary insight were at play. I shared that Mary said she and Yeshua were sacred partners, or "holy husband and wife." I also said that Mary was a priestess in the temple of Isis, where she was prepared for her sacred relationship with Yeshua. I explained that Mary's focus was on strengthening our relationship to our bodies, sexuality, and emotions as the foundation for living in our hearts and incarnating the Divine Feminine. The host seemed happy with all this information.

By the end of the afternoon, I was tired from the huge amount of energy that had been running through me. Later that evening, I received a call from a woman going through a rough time, which she attributed to the energies of the day. She wanted a channeled session so she could consult with Yeshua. I told her I'd be available in a couple of days. Nevertheless, her call started me wondering what other people had experienced during the day. I called a few friends, but got only answering machines.

I considered calling Tony, but hesitated, not sure whether communication with him would support me emotionally in the midst of our separation. Finally I realized that today was a once in a lifetime occasion and Tony was one of the few people in my life whose opinion about spiritual matters I valued, due to his spiritual maturity. Then I called. It turned out his experience had been similar to mine. "I felt the energies of the day as very strong and full of light," he related. "I spent the day going slow, being with myself, meditating at twelve minutes after twelve."

It felt so good talking with him that I decided to take a chance and ask him about an idea that had occurred to me. "I've been thinking about Mary's instruction," I began, "and wondering how to carry out the advanced practices she's bringing forth now that we're not together anymore. Would you be open to completing the remainder of the practices together as energy exchanges? We could stay fully clothed and engage them without physical love-making."

"I'd like to do that," he replied. "I value all we've gone through in our relationship and sexuality, and I want to support the completion of this work with Mary."

It became suddenly clear to me this would be a perfect arrangement. Any couple working at this level would need to first learn the practices in a purely energetic form before applying them in their sexuality. It would be too difficult to learn them while making love because the pull to the familiar physical patterns would be too strong. The advanced practices are really about transitioning from physical lovemaking to energetic lovemaking in a fourth-dimensional manner.

Emboldened by Tony's receptivity to my idea, I shared a second thought with him, saying. "I was envisioning doing our practice sessions as an intensive, perhaps meeting daily and completing the culminating session on December 21. What do you think about that?"

"I think it's a great idea," he affirmed.

I felt excited and hopeful, while also curious about the outcome: *Would the practices be as powerful and effective without physical love-making? Would we enjoy them as much? And what would it be like to spend time together in this more restrained way?*

We set our first session for December 14—two days away.

FORTY-EIGHT

Rising Serpents

*O*n the morning of my first practice session with Tony, I asked Mary for further guidance. She responded instantly.

Thank you for inviting me to communicate with you. It has been a while since we have spoken. You have needed time to integrate the changes you have gone through with Tony and be ready to embark on the next phase of our process. I commend you highly for your service and unrelenting perseverance in this endeavor, and I thank you. Without someone living the teachings and recording their experiences, this work would not be accessible to others. There are many who desire this instruction and who will be greatly supported by it.

Your higher self has guided you well in coming up with a solution to moving forward with the work while not being in an intimate relationship with Tony. Following guidance from one's higher self is required to truly engage the advanced-level practices of sacred sexuality. This is part of the transition that humanity is in altogether at the current time of growing beyond gurus and teachers in order to find one's own way. Although others may have guidance you can learn from, you are ultimately in charge of your own growth, development, and choices. Through your higher self, you will be guided to make the choices that are right for you.

This level of maturity allows you to attain a very fine level of balance, where you respect and value the truth as it is offered to you from apparent outside sources. But it must always be checked and validated by your own truth from your higher self. Much of the truth and wisdom you need will be provided to you directly through your higher self, and it will not be necessary to engage outside sources.

Receiving help directly from your higher self will not isolate you from others, nor will it put you in a position of conflict or struggle in relationship to others. If what you are receiving from others is truth, your connection with your higher self will support you in attaining harmony, openheartedness, and connection with those others. If you are not being supported in those ways, then what you have been taking as truth from outside sources is probably not so.

Having a stronger relationship to your higher self is all part of the new disposition of the fourth-dimensional consciousness. And it is aligned and in sync with the higher practices of sacred sexuality, which you will now be engaging.

And so, my dear one, your solution of how to work with Tony is excellent. You have rightly surmised that this is the approach most people will need to take in learning this material. It is necessary to initially practice the advanced sacred sexuality exercises with minimal physical engagement so the energetic aspects can be optimally cultivated.

In the arena of sexuality, the physical impulses and tendencies, along with the third-dimensional instinctual drives, are quite powerful, as most of you are aware. This is what has allowed your species to survive through reproduction. They have also allowed you to have a full experiential understanding of sexuality at the purely physical level. That learning phase is now complete for humanity. Those who are most mature and spiritually developed are longing for something more evolved and pure in the realm of sexuality. This is evidence of a readiness on the part of humanity to begin to learn, master, and embody the practices based in fourth-dimensional reality that I have been sharing with you.

Two advanced practices to cultivate at this time in humanity's unfoldment are the double serpents practice [see figure 48-1] and, in its more advanced form, the four serpents practice [see figure 48-2].[1] You have already received instruction in these practices through prior communications from me and from Isis, as well as your own remembering of them. As such, you will be able to share this information with Tony and engage them together. I will, of course, be here to help and guide you as necessary, but I trust you and know you as fully competent and developed in these high arts.

With love and gratitude,
I AM Mary Magdalene

I was well aware of the practices Mary was referring to. I had first engaged the double serpents some years earlier, later adding in the four serpents. I considered these practices the pinnacle of the Egyptian sacred sexuality system, and they seemed the perfect completion to all we'd gone through up to that point. I looked forward to sharing both of them with Tony.

Later that afternoon, I got a call from Tony. "I'm really backed up with projects I need to complete before Christmas," he told me. "I want to spend time with you, as we talked about, but I'm going to have to postpone it a few days. Will that work for you?"

"Actually, it would be a relief for me, too," I replied. "I need more time for work right now. Let's just stay in touch and see what happens."

I wondered if we were both nervous about spending time together again. I trusted whatever would occur and felt uncharacteristically patient about allowing events to unfold naturally. As it turned out, nearly a week would pass before Tony and I got together again.

Figure 48-1. DOUBLE

1. Awaken and arouse your sexual energy, either by yourself or with a partner. If you are with a partner, the practice is begun after you are already joined in sexual union.

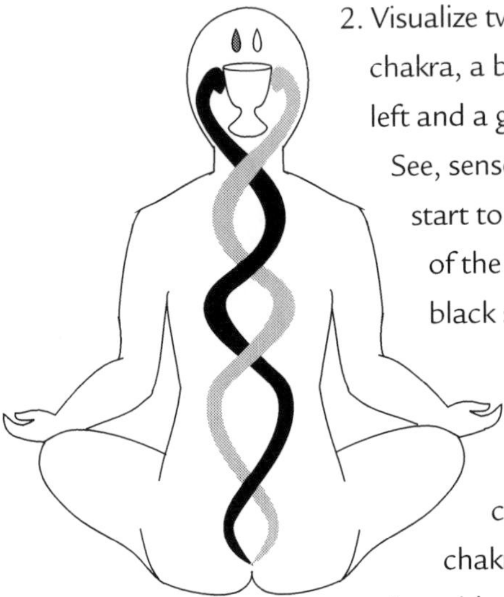

2. Visualize two serpents at your root chakra, a black serpent on the left and a gold one on the right. See, sense, or feel the serpents start to rise on opposite sides of the spinal column—the black serpent on the left and the gold one on the right. See, sense, or feel the two serpents crossing at your sacral chakra and continuing to rise, with the gold one now on the left and the black one on the right. See, sense, or feel them crossing again at your solar plexus and heart chakras respectively, continuing to rise on opposite sides, and crossing for the final time at your throat chakra. Finally, see, sense, or feel the black snake rising from your throat chakra on the left once again and the gold snake on the right once again to the center of your head, where they face each other with their heads down, maintaining a slight distance between the tops of their heads.

SERPENTS PRACTICE

3. Breathe into the serpents until you feel them writhing and coming alive. Allow your body to move with this energization.

4. Shift your focus to the center of your head and see, sense, or feel a chalice held between the serpents' heads.

5. Shift your focus to your solar plexus chakra, then see, sense, or feel a brilliant sun there, known as the "sun of Ra."[2] With each exhalation, silently intone "Ra" as you breathe energy into this ball of fire. Allow your body to move naturally with this breathing and silent toning. See, sense, or feel the sun slowly ascend your spinal column, through the chalice, to your crown chakra.

6. When the sun of Ra reaches your crown chakra, orgasm occurs. As you orgasm, place your awareness at your crown chakra.

7. Notice as two drops of nectarous energy are released from your crown chakra into the chalice.[3] The red drop released from the left side of your crown is the Feminine essence. The white drop released from the right side of your crown is the Masculine essence.

8. Allow the drops to mix in the chalice. Be aware of a sweet taste at the back of your throat or of light in your head, and a feeling of ecstasy. As soon as the ecstasy rises, focus your awareness on your energy body, which will then spread the ecstasy through your whole physical and energetic self for strengthening, energizing, rejuvenation, and transformation.

Figure 48-2. FOUR SERPENTS PRACTICE

Together with your partner, follow the instructions for the double serpents practice, with this variation: Raise your serpents through your partner's body, as your partner raises their serpents through your body. Continue doing steps 3 through 6 through each other's body until the release of the nectarous drops, which you each experience in your own body. The rest of the practice is done in relation to your own body.

FORTY-NINE

Galactic Alignment

As December 21 approached, I began feeling the energy of the galactic alignment intensifying. I experienced increasing periods of great tiredness, sleeping more and functioning in a kind of hibernation mode, interspersed with times of being highly energized and accomplishing a great deal effortlessly.

I considered the day before 12/21/12 as the start of an empowered three-day window of spiritual transformation. To make the most of this period of opportunity, I decided to go on retreat at my home for all three days, holding space for most anything to occur.

Whatever might happen—whether untold cataclysms would befall us or the heavens would open and welcome us to new realms of paradise—I felt anxious and sad about facing the event alone. It had been over a week since Tony and I had decided to complete the advanced practices energetically, and we hadn't yet managed to get together for a practice session. But I knew he was the one I wanted to be with. I felt safe with Tony. So I asked him if he would spend the three days with me. To my great relief and happiness, he said he'd like to do that.

According to some spiritual teachers, the peak energy was

expected to occur at 4:11 a.m. on December 21. One Mayan spiritual teacher described an eight-minute gateway that would open at that time, in which humanity would experience being in the higher dimensions. He urged people to write down their experiences afterward and remember them so they wouldn't recede, like a dream, into oblivion. Other teachers predicted that some or all of humanity would transition into a higher dimension either on December 21 or shortly thereafter.

I wasn't sure what that three-day period would bring or whether the effects would be immediate or more long range. What I did know was that I wanted to spend the three days engaging the advanced sacred sexuality practices, which to me seemed the most auspicious way of aligning with the energies of the fourth dimension. And I wanted to do it with Tony.

I'd come down with a cold the day before our planned retreat, which was unusual for me. My throat started burning at the very spot where I activate the connection between my Divine Feminine and Masculine in meditation. I wondered if the burning signaled a final purification of internal blocks, allowing me to fully connect my inner Feminine and Masculine. I also thought being sick was opening me to better receive the transformative energies of this auspicious time by moving me out of my usual physical vitality into a lighter, more energy-based state. My plan was to drink juices and eat raw foods, and thereby get through the cold more quickly and easefully.

Tony arrived for the retreat at midday on December 20 while I was taking a hot soak in the tub. I came out to find him relaxing on the sofa. We greeted each other and embraced, then moved into my bedroom.

"I think we should be clear about our intentions and agreements for this retreat," I began. "I want to honor this time in whatever way seems most favorable for aligning with the energies available.

If it feels right, I would like to engage sacred sexuality as a purely energetic practice, without physical lovemaking." Tony agreed unreservedly.

We took off our clothes down to our underwear and lay next to each other. I suggested we begin by connecting our chakras. We started at the heart chakra. On the inhalation, we breathed energy into our own hearts. As we exhaled, we mingled our energies. After several minutes of not feeling a strong connection, I said, "I sense you're holding your energy back. Are you afraid of getting turned on?"

"Yes, I think I am."

"I think it's fine if we get turned on," I said. "We can just experience and relax into whatever feelings we have, without acting on them. We can also talk about what we're feeling with each other. If we want to act, we can discuss that together." Tony agreed with everything I said. Our interchange seemed to relax him.

We went back to the chakra breathing practice, but our connection still didn't feel alive. I had another intuition come up. I told Tony, "I'm guessing you might have some pain in your heart that you don't want to feel. Do you have pain in relation to me?"

"Yes, I do," he confirmed. "When you told me you were going to start dating again, I felt hurt, like I was just one of your boyfriends." I sensed the release of tension in him as he expressed this, and I celebrated his openness in sharing something so vulnerable.

"There's no way you could be just one of my boyfriends," I told him. "I love you and have a completely unique relationship with you. I'd like to be partners with you, but you aren't choosing to do that with me."

"I know that," he acknowledged. Again our talking seemed to release his feelings and open him up.

Finally we were ready to begin. We returned to the breathing exercise, and now it was fully alive and strong. Starting at the heart, we breathed down to each chakra. At the sacral chakra, we experienced powerful energetic orgasms, with the sexual energy moving us from undulations to spasms of liquid bliss. When we got to the root chakra, I wanted to be closer physically so we could have a full exchange of energy. We shifted positions, and the energy mushroomed between us. I told Tony, "I'm really feeling like I want to wrap my legs around you."

"I was feeling the same thing!" he exclaimed.

We changed positions again, to one with Tony on top of me, my legs embracing him, and the tip of his lingam at my pearl. The energy kept growing, along with our desire to fully merge our bodies. Finally Tony said, "I want to be inside you," and he took off both our underwear. He lay back down on top of me, and we stayed in stillness, feeling the energy moving between us. As the energy grew, my resolve to not make love faded away.

Tony started moving, and I said, "Don't push. Let the movement come from our energy, not from initiating it physically." We lay together for quite a while with the energy getting stronger and stronger. Finally his lingam was right at the opening of my yoni, and he slipped in just a tiny bit. I said, "Let's relax here," and we did. Before we knew it, Tony was deep inside me, as though the energy had pulled us together. We continued to make love, moving very little, letting the energy lead us.

The powerful force between us continued to build, and we had several orgasms together. Then we stopped and remained very still. Slowly the energy built again, and we became very passionate, yet with little movement, flowing in a potent dance of eros.

I could feel a soreness inside me. Tony said he could feel the spot, too. We stayed motionless for a time with him still inside me. Then he went deeper, and I shifted into a whole new level of feeling, grabbing him at the back of his pelvis and pulling him strongly to me. We orgasmed many times, eventually coming back to stillness.

I asked Tony if he'd put some healing gel on my yoni. He sensually spread the gel around the outside of my yoni, then went inside me with it. Finding it deliciously erotic, I started orgasming again. We enjoyed that for quite a while until I pulled Tony back on top of me and we returned once more to making love.

Finally we moved into nesting, with Tony holding me and stroking me. As usual, this part of our lovemaking was incredibly sweet and bonding.

After a late lunch, we were ready to explore the double serpents practice. I reviewed the steps with Tony; then we decided to do it individually as a guided meditation, with me talking us through it. Tony sat on a chair so his spine could be fully erect, and I sat on the bed.

I originally intended to only lead us through the first step of the practice, the raising of the serpents from the root chakra to the center of the head. But after we'd completed that, I spontaneously kept going—through the energizing of the serpents, connecting with the chalice in the center of the head, raising the sun of Ra from the solar plexus to the crown, releasing the nectarous energy into the chalice, and drawing the ecstasy into the energy body. It all unfolded effortlessly, and I could energetically feel Tony following along, each step of the way.

Afterward, Tony said, "I think I'll need to do that a few more times before I really have it." Then we both were tired and fell asleep for about an hour.

Intending to join people around the world who would be meditating at the time the galactic alignment was to occur, we planned to go to bed early so we could wake up at 3:30 a.m. and be meditating by 4:11. We managed to go to bed at 9:00 p.m. but woke up almost hourly thereafter. The night had a very unusual quality to it, as though time had stopped and all of life had become totally still and peaceful. It seemed to take forever to reach 3:30 a.m.

Finally the designated hour arrived. We woke easily and were meditating by 4:00 a.m. I focused on myself and all beings going through the ascension in whatever way would be for the highest good of all involved. I didn't notice anything particularly unusual other than a light fluttering sensation in my heart, which brought the phrase "fairy dust" to my mind. I meditated until 4:30, at which point I felt complete. Returning to bed, I fell fast asleep.

Tony continued meditating until 5:00 a.m. before rejoining me in bed, where we both slept soundly and woke up hours later feeling very happy. We spent a long time snuggling in bed, enjoying being physically close. Both of us acknowledged that though we hadn't planned to include intercourse in our time together we were glad we had.

"When I opened my eyes after the meditation," Tony shared, "the first thing I saw was your vacant cushion. I immediately thought, *She's vanished—gone into the higher realms!* Then I noticed you were in bed." We both laughed.

When I told him about my meditation experience, he reported, "Mine wasn't very different either, other than evoking a strong feeling of peace."

At noon we went out for brunch, sitting beside each other in a booth as we always had. The day seemed to fly by, as though time was making up for its extreme slowness the night before. Tony left in the late afternoon to run some errands, giving me space to rest. In the evening we enjoyed the movie *Avatar* and then fell happily asleep.

FIFTY

Fulfillment

*T*ony and I woke up together at 3:33 a.m., holding each other close. He whispered, "I'd like to be making love."

"Me, too," I concurred. "But I'm also aware of my resolve to not engage in sex unless we've agreed to be in a committed life partnership. Even though we didn't follow that a couple days ago, I still need that boundary to protect myself. I've come to accept that my emotional and energetic bodies believe I'm in a dedicated partnership any time I open myself physically to another person. If that's not the case, sooner or later I get hurt."

"I understand," Tony said. I felt us shift into a more relaxed space even as we continued to hold each other and allow our sexual attraction to arise.

"I'd like to hear more about why you don't want to be married," I said.

"I've been looking at that myself," he replied, "and I don't feel clear."

"My guess is that you feel afraid to enter into another relationship," I suggested, "either because of being burned out from your marriage or because you want to enjoy the freedom of following your own desires without having to cooperate and coordinate with anyone else."

"Both are true," he acknowledged. "But I miss being in relationship when I'm alone. I'm especially burned out from caretaking my ex-wife and yet I feel kind of hopeless about extricating myself from that role. I've been thinking of seeing a therapist to help me get past the fear I feel about being in relationship."

I felt joy welling up within me, as this was the first time I'd heard Tony say he would seek help with his situation. "I notice that regardless of the challenges coming up between us," I remarked, "when we talk about what's going on, sharing our feelings and thoughts all the way to the end, I'm consistently returned to a place of unconditional love. I so value that." We both observed that the energy channels between us were once again fully open and we felt turned on and strongly drawn to each other.

Yet we were both relaxed, honoring my commitment to avoid engaging in physical sex. It was pleasurable to feel our sexual aliveness and attraction, and yet be able to rest in it without transgressing our new boundaries.

Tony continued stroking me, but I could feel a shift in him. "Are you feeling sad?" I asked.

"Yes," he said. Then he added, "I don't feel ready to talk about it."

"I think we'll both feel better if we do," I countered.

"I'm sad about us not continuing our sexual relationship," he said. "Are you sad about that?"

I checked in with myself and realized I wasn't. "Actually I'm not at this moment," I shared. "I'm embracing the inner wholeness I feel from taking care of myself." We continued holding each other and then slipped back into sleep.

We woke up much later, still feeling very connected. After embracing for a while, I asked Tony, "Would you like to engage the serpents practice energetically?"

"Yes," he said.

We reviewed the instructions and agreed to first raise the double serpents through our own bodies and then, moving into the ultimate form of the four serpents, raise our own serpents through each other's body.

While lying next to each other, I could feel Tony's lingam through my panties, right at the entrance to my yoni. Already the sexual energy was flowing intensely between us. We started by breathing into our root chakras. I guided us verbally in moving our serpents up along the spinal column, unaware of how I'd know when they had reached each chakra, but it turned out to be extremely clear. By the time the serpent energy had reached our throat chakras, I realized I was visualizing the serpents moving through my body in reverse, the way they would be if Tony had been raising his serpents through my body. Simultaneously, I was seeing my serpents moving through Tony's body. I told him this, and he said, "I'm having the same experience." Without even trying, we had effortlessly moved into the four serpents practice!

We then breathed into the serpents, and they immediately came to life, writhing powerfully. Next, we visualized the chalice in the center of our heads and brought our third eye chakras together in stillness.

Once the chalice felt clearly in place, we shifted our focus to our solar plexus chakras, feeling and visualizing a ball of fire there, the sun of Ra. Intoning a silent "Ra" on our exhalations, we experienced the sun rising up through our chakras. By our third exhalation, it had reached our crown chakras, causing us to explode in waves of orgasm. Focusing our awareness at our crown chakras, we allowed the orgasmic energy to charge our energy bodies. Then we experienced the descent of the two drops into the chalice at the center of our heads, now absorbing this into our energy bodies.

Finally we came to rest nesting together, blown away by what had happened. Simultaneously extremely energized, relaxed, and open, we vibrated for a long time with the energy moving through us. I felt as though we had been gently carried into the fourth dimension and were floating in that marvelous space together.

The entire process seemed to have taken very little time, but after looking at his watch, Tony noted, "An hour has passed since we began." The time distortion wasn't the only unusual characteristic of this practice. Unlike other occasions of lovemaking, I felt thoroughly satisfied after one shared orgasm. This was clearly a very different type of orgasm than any I'd experienced before.

"It was really incredible," Tony declared. "Are there other advanced practices?"

"This was *the* advanced practice," I clarified, "and we just graduated with flying colors!"

We reflected on our course, beginning with the Tantric wave, moving on to the partner ankh, and now fulfilling the four serpents practice—an ecstatic ride spanning more than four months. And now it really did seem to have come to completion.

We had an invitation to get together with friends that night, but during the afternoon I took a nosedive and suddenly started to feel much worse. By early evening I was only slightly better, and we both agreed I should stay home and rest. Alone once again, I prepared my bed for sleeping and started to cry, realizing, *Tony isn't coming back.* I'd come to an ending—of our three days together, of our sublime union . . . and of my hope for us becoming life partners. Suddenly I understood why I hadn't felt well that afternoon.

Through my tears, I flashed back to when I first met Tony. *Did Spirit guide me to Community Church that first morning of my arrival in Santa Fe to meet Tony?* I asked myself. *Has it all been planned from the start so I could go through this process with him? He was a perfect fit—a match for me spiritually, open-minded, sensitive to energy, valuing growth, strong and secure enough in himself to open to a powerful woman, strong and secure enough in himself to allow me to be a woman with him.* I concluded that he was indeed a gift from Spirit and I was blessed to have had the chance to live Mary's teachings with him.

FIFTY-ONE

It Is Done

*S*ix days later, Mary came once more, bringing closure to our profound journey together in the realms of sacred sexuality.

Greetings and blessings, my sweet soul sister,

You have been through a difficult time. I feel you and send you love in your pain and tender troubles. I also thank you for going through this, along with all else we have gone through together. I thank you for persevering. You are on your path, and, as you know, this is a part of it. I acknowledge you and commend you for your dedication and unswerving devotion to this calling.

The information you have received is now complete, as is your work with Tony in embodying it and demonstrating it in life. You have both done an excellent job of manifesting the wisdom I have imparted. All is now in place for this treasured information to be shared with your world.

I know that you have wondered if you and Tony were brought together simply to do this work. It is more accurate to say that you both chose to do this work together. Tony has not chosen to continue on with you in this way, and you are going through the pain of releasing the bonds of closeness you have forged together. I hold you with care and tenderness as you go though the release of your heart-closeness with him. I also trust that this, too, will lead you to the next portion of your path in God. I do not say that to distract you from your pain or grieving, but rather to support you in trusting the process and opening fully to it, including experiencing your feelings of loss. When you are in pain, it is often easy to lose sight of the bigger picture. It can be helpful to have others who are holding you in that larger view and reminding you of it.

I celebrate that this information about sacred sexuality can now be made available to all people. This is a valuable contribution to humanity's evolution into higher states of being. I thank you for all you have done to support the dissemination of this material. You are an important part of bringing this treasured information into the light of day.

Now I wish to take you with me once more to the Sea of Galilee. Let us join hands, traveling freely and swiftly, beyond the confines of space. Arriving in this distant land, where the shining sun warms the earth, we descend upon the waters, buoyed by the swells of the sea. As we walk upon the water together, allow yourself to be cleansed of all worries and concerns, all heartaches and pains, all sense of separation from your fullest embrace with God. Know that you are loved by your Father-Mother God most fully, held as their beloved child. They will continue to direct you, as they always have, and you will be fine. In your unity with God, you are whole and all is well. You are loved, and you are love. I love you, and I rejoice in your love. All is well.

Blessings and love,
I AM Mary Magdalene

As Mary spoke her last words, I felt her drawing me into unity with Mother-Father God. I seemed to be continuously expanding, growing large in God. At the same time, Mary was moving farther and farther away. I heard her voice coming from an increasing distance, as though she was leaving me with God. As I heard her final words, I felt both sad and peacefully whole. The phrase appearing in my consciousness was "It is done."

Afterword: Continuing the Journey

THANK YOU FOR SHARING this journey with me. I hope this book has inspired you, deepened your understanding of sacred sexuality, and given you concrete tools for your growth.

For those who want to continue learning in this arena, I strongly recommend attending an introductory sacred sexuality workshop. As you've probably gathered, the essence of this practice involves connecting with energy and learning to direct it in new pathways. This is generally learned most easily through an experiential workshop, guided by a skilled teacher. Just as you probably wouldn't try to learn to dance or sing by merely reading about those techniques, this process is similar. Yet once you discover the basics within yourself, a book *can* help to build on that foundation.

If you're interested in studying with me, I offer both workshops and individual instruction for singles and couples in the areas of communication, relationships, and sacred sexuality. I also offer channeled readings to connect with Mary Magdalene, your personal guides, or other beings of light. You can learn more about the workshops and sessions I offer at www.mercedeskirkel.com.

Many people ask me if they can practice sacred sexuality as a single person, and my answer is an emphatic "Yes!" Many of the activities I've described in the book can be done as a solo practice. Learning to connect with your own energy and move it in the ways described is a path of union with the Divine in and of itself, as well as an essential step for moving toward sacred sexuality with a partner. In addition to working with your own energy as an inner practice (similar in many ways to the energy practices of yoga, tai chi, chi gong, or other martial arts), you can also find a friend with whom to engage the verbal and energy exchanges. This can be done as a clothes-on, nonsexual activity, setting whatever boundaries you need for your comfort and safety.

The last thought I wish to leave you with is this: I absolutely celebrate everything I went through with Tony—the love, the ecstasy, the growth, the sadness, the loss—all of it. I've come to realize that our coming together wasn't about me finding the "perfect partner" or having our relationship "work out" in the way I had in my mind. I'm deeply grateful that we were able to serve Mary Magdalene as vehicles for bringing her teaching of sacred sexuality forward at this time. Beyond that, our relationship was an exquisite piece in my path of reunion with God and All That Is. I believe that if we find another to share any part of that divine odyssey with us, we are truly blessed.

Notes

Mary Magdalene and Her Current Mission

1. "Yeshua" was the Aramaic/Hebrew name for Jesus. Aramaic was the common language spoken in Judea at the time of Jesus's incarnation.

2. Mary Magdalene uses the term *God* interchangeably with *the Divine, Mother-Father-God, Father-Mother-God, God-Goddess, Source, Oneness,* and *Supreme Creator.* She sees God as encompassing both the Divine Feminine and the Divine Masculine, the transcendental, and all of physical and energetic manifestation. A thorough explanation of her understanding of the nature of God can be found in *Mary Magdalene Beckons* by Mercedes Kirkel.

3. Mercedes Kirkel, *Mary Magdalene Beckons: Join the River of Love* (Santa Fe, NM: Into the Heart Creations, 2012), 77 and 80–81.

4. Tantra refers to a body of ancient Indian spiritual practices that included sexuality as an avenue of oneness with the Divine.

5. Kirkel, *Mary Magdalene Beckons,* 268–269.

Chapter 1

1. *Kundalini* is a Sanskrit term for the life-force energy that rests in its dormant state at the base of the spine. In both yoga and sacred sexuality, practices are engaged for awakening this energy, allowing it to move up the spine to support spiritual transformation.

2. Mary Magdalene uses the term *God* interchangeably with *the Divine, Mother-Father-God, Father-Mother-God, God-Goddess, Source, Oneness,* and *Supreme Creator.* She sees God as encompassing both the Divine Feminine and the Divine Masculine, the transcendental, and all of physical and energetic manifestation. A thorough explanation of her understanding of the nature of God can be found in *Mary Magdalene Beckons* by Mercedes Kirkel.

Chapter 3

1. Chakras are energy centers in the body. The seven primary chakras are contained within the central channel, which runs along the spinal line from the perineum to the crown of the head. The function of each of the chakras is described in figure 3-1.

Chapter 4

1. My mantra was a blessing prayer I'd created for myself and used regularly to strengthen my practice of divine communion.

2. The fourth dimension is the plane of reality above the third dimension and is energetically rather than physically based. The fourth dimension is described in detail in *Mary Magdalene Beckons* by Mercedes Kirkel.

Chapter 10

1. The *merkaba* is a part of our subtle body, or light body, which helps individuals move from one dimension to another. Its star tetrahedron shape surrounds the human body, while the full merkaba field extends out approximately fifty-five feet and has a UFO-like flying saucer shape.

Chapter 12

1. *Inner divine qualities* is a term Mary uses to refer to the internal qualities at the root of all emotions. These qualities are shared by all people and constitute the inner divinity of humanity. A thorough explanation of humanity's inner divine qualities can be found in *Mary Magdalene Beckons* by Mercedes Kirkel.

Chapter 13

1. *Pranayama* is a Sanskrit term for breathing practices that develop the life-force energy and support spiritual growth.

2. Ouija board is a game that involves two people placing their fingers lightly on a disc and asking a question they want answered. The players allow the disc to move over the game board, independent of any intention or effort on their part. The answer to the question is revealed through the letters or symbols on the game board upon which the disc comes to rest.

Chapter 15

1. The ankh breathing practice is described in chapter 25 and illustrated in figure 25-1. It is named after an ancient Egyptian symbol generally associated with eternal life.

2. A mandala is a spiritual image that uses geometric patterns and symbols to represent the cosmos and other metaphysical concepts.

Chapter 17

1. In the book *The Magdalen Manuscript* by Tom Kenyon and Judi Sion, Mary Magdalene describes a practice of "nesting" after lovemaking, in which the man remains close to the woman through touch and physical contact as both partners verbalize their sensations and emotions. Nesting is considered especially important for the man because through this exchange he continues to absorb essential Feminine energies from the woman.

Chapter 20

1. The Urantia teaching is a series of spiritual messages that were published in the early twentieth century describing the nature of God and the cosmos, the purpose of life, and the history of the Earth from its creation to the present.

Chapter 25

1. Mystery schools are institutions dedicated to esoteric spiritual knowledge and practices. In ancient times, a mystery school was generally a secret organization in which information was shared only with initiates. *Ascension* refers to the process of spiritual transformation that leads beings of the third dimension into residing at progressively higher dimensions of reality.

2. In sacred sexuality, men learn that ejaculation and orgasm are two distinct processes that can be separated. Through practice, men can experience orgasms without ejaculating, allowing them to have multiple orgasms and enjoy extended lovemaking.

3. Orbs are spheres of light, often showing up in photographs, that many people believe are higher-dimensional beings "visiting" the third dimension.

Chapter 27

1. *Yab-yum* is the name of a lovemaking position in Indian Tantra, in which the man sits cross-legged with his partner sitting on his lap, facing him. The position is illustrated in figure 27-1.

Chapter 34

1. The causal body is one of six bodies that comprise the whole self in the third and fourth dimensions. The other five bodies are the physical, etheric (or energetic), emotional, mental, and spiritual bodies. The causal body is the seat of the soul and one's sense of identity as an individuated being, including all memories from previous incarnations.

Chapter 39

1. Shiva and Shakti are a pair of divine lovers in the Indian tradition, representing the union of the Divine Masculine and Feminine.

Chapter 41

1. The G-spot, or Goddess spot, is a point on the front wall of the vagina, where a woman tends to hold cellular memories of sexual trauma and wounding. It's also a place of potent sexual pleasure for many women, especially after receiving healing there.

Chapter 48

1. The practices of the double serpents and four serpents are advanced Egyptian sacred sexuality practices. For a step-by-step description of these practices, see figures 48-1 and 48-2. A full discussion of these practices can be found in *The Magdalen Manuscript* by Tom Kenyon and Judi Sion.

2. Ra is the ancient Egyptian sun god.

3. The drops of nectarous energy are a substance that is released from the crown of the head during orgasm in the practices of the double serpents and four serpents. These drops are also known as *amrita* in the Indian tradition, which is translated as "nectar of immortality." A deeper discussion of these drops can be found in *The Magdalen Manuscript* by Tom Kenyon and Judy Sion, in which they are referred to as serpentine drops.

Terms and Their Meanings

12/21/12—The date of December 21, 2012, was believed by many to be the end of the Mayan calendar, the beginning of a new age, and/or a time when the Earth was passing through the center of the galaxy, which was referred to as the galactic alignment. Numerous spiritual traditions and prophecies seemed to corroborate the importance of that date as being a time of either great destruction or profound transformation, or in some cases both.

Ankh—Ancient Egyptian symbol of a cross with a loop on top, which is generally associated with eternal life.

Ascension—Spiritual transformation that leads beings of the third dimension into residing at progressively higher dimensions of reality.

Central channel—The energetic column that runs along the spinal line from the root chakra at the base of the spine through the crown chakra at the top of the head.

Chakras—Energy centers in the body. The seven primary chakras are contained within the central channel, which runs along the spinal line from the perineum to the crown of the head. The function of each of the chakras is described in figure 3-1.

Fourth dimension—The plane of reality above the third dimension; it is energetically rather than physically based. The fourth dimension is described in detail in *Mary Magdalene Beckons* by Mercedes Kirkel.

God—Mary Magdalene uses the term *God* interchangeably with *the Divine, Mother-Father-God, Father-Mother-God, God-Goddess, Source, Oneness,* and *Supreme Creator.* She sees God as encompassing both the Divine Feminine and the Divine Masculine, the transcendental, and all of physical and energetic manifestation. A thorough explanation of her understanding of the nature of God can be found in *Mary Magdalene Beckons* by Mercedes Kirkel.

Inner divine qualities—A term Mary uses to refer to the internal qualities at the root of all emotions. These qualities are shared by all people and constitute the inner divinity of humanity. Examples of inner divine qualities include autonomy, authenticity, respect, love, understanding, play, rest, connection, and trust. A thorough explanation of humanity's inner divine qualities can be found in *Mary Magdalene Beckons* by Mercedes Kirkel.

Isis—An ancient Egyptian goddess who was worshipped as the representation of the Divine Feminine, especially as wife and mother.

Kundalini—Sanskrit term for the life-force energy that rests in its dormant state at the base of the spine. In both yoga and sacred sexuality, practices are engaged for awakening this energy, allowing it to rise up the spine to support spiritual transformation.

Lingam—Sanskrit term for a man's penis; literally "wand of light."

Mantra—A blessing prayer that is repeated frequently to support a person's practice of divine communion.

Mary Magdalene—The sacred partner of Yeshua (Jesus), embodying the Divine Feminine in relation to his Divine Masculine and joining him in spiritual service and teaching for the sake of humanity's spiritual evolution.

Merkaba—Part of our subtle body, or light body, that helps individuals move from one dimension to another. Its star tetrahedron shape surrounds the human body, while the full merkaba field extends out approximately fifty-five feet and has a UFO-like flying saucer shape.

Nesting—A practice that occurs after lovemaking, in which the man remains close to the woman through touch and physical contact as both partners verbalize their sensations and emotions. Nesting is considered especially important for the man because throughout this time he continues to absorb essential Feminine energies from the woman.

Prana—Sanskrit term for life force, or internal energy.

Sekhem—Ancient Egyptian term for life force, or internal energy, that moves along the central channel.

Tantra—A body of ancient Indian spiritual practices that included sexuality as an avenue of oneness with the Divine.

Tantrica—A practitioner of Tantra.

Temple of Isis—Ancient Egyptian temple complexes dedicated to worship of the goddess Isis.

Yab-yum—The name of a lovemaking position in Indian Tantra, in which the man sits cross-legged with his partner sitting on his lap, facing him. See figure 27-1.

Yeshua—Aramaic/Hebrew name for Jesus.

Yoni—Tantric term for a woman's vagina; literally, "sacred space."

Sacred Sexuality Resources

Anand, Margo. *The Art of Sexual Ecstasy: The Path of Sacred Sexuality for Western Lovers*. New York: Jeremy P. Tarcher, 1990.

Chia, Mantak, and Douglas Abrams. *The Multi-Orgasmic Man: How Any Man Can Experience Multiple Orgasms and Dramatically Enhance His Sexual Relationship*. San Francisco: HarperOne, 2009.

Chia, Mantak, and Maneewan Chia, Douglas Abrams, and Rachel Cralton Abrams, MD. *The Multi-Orgasmic Couple: How Couples Can Dramatically Enhance Their Pleasure, Intimacy, and Health*. San Francisco: HarperOne, 2010.

Kenyon, Tom, and Judi Sion. *The Magdalen Manuscript: The Alchemies of Horus & The Sex Magic of Isis*. Boulder, CO: Sounds True, 2006.

Kirkel, Mercedes. *Mary Magdalene Beckons: Join the River of Love*. Santa Fe, NM: Into the Heart Creations, 2012.

Riley, Kerry, with Diane Riley. *Tantric Secrets for Men: What Every Woman Will Want Her Man to Know about Enhancing Sexual Ecstasy*. Rochester, VT: Destiny Books, 2002.

About the Author

MERCEDES KIRKEL is a multi-award-winning author and channel for Mary Magdalene. In the summer of 2010, Mary Magdalene began coming to Mercedes daily, giving extraordinary messages for humanity's evolution and spiritual growth. That was the birth of her first book, *Mary Magdalene Beckons: Join the River of Love*. Since then, Mary Magdalene has continued to communicate through Mercedes, delivering illuminating messages about uniting with God and the sacred partnership of the Divine Feminine and Masculine.

Based out of Santa Fe, New Mexico, and the San Francisco Bay Area, Mercedes offers workshops and private sessions locally, online, and via phone. She's also available to travel to other locations by request. Her specialties include heart-based life-and-relationships coaching, guidance from Mary Magdalene and other beings of light, Akashic healing and soul-path guidance, Light-Filled Intimacy™ instruction, and spiritual instruction and support.

To learn more about the author and her work, please visit www.mercedeskirkel.com.

To sign up for the INTO THE HEART newsletter
with ongoing messages from Mary Magdalene, go to:
www.mercedeskirkel.com

To receive a free LIGHT-FILLED INTIMACY™
guided meditation recording from Mercedes Kirkel, go to:
www.sublime-union.com

To purchase additional copies of *Sublime Union*
in book, e-book, or audiobook format, please visit:

www.sublime-union.com

Also by Mercedes Kirkel

Mary Magdalene Beckons: Join the River of Love

Book One of The Magdalene Teachings

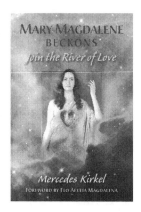

In this multi-award-winning book of spiritual
guidance, Mary Magdalene illuminates the
sacred partnership of the Divine Feminine
and Masculine, including how our bodies,
sexuality, and emotions are pathways to God.

"*Mary Magdalene Beckons* offers helpful insights for creating balance and
harmony between the Masculine and Feminine within all of us."

—John Gray, author of *Men Are from Mars, Women Are from Venus*

"One of the most profound books of our day."

—Flo Aeveia Magdalena, author of *I Remember Union*

"If you want to hear the real voice of Mary Magdalene, buy this book."

—Stuart Wilson and Joanna Prentis, authors of *The Magdalene*

"An outstanding spiritual self-help book . . . I felt love and surrender, and
forgiveness and an acceptance of myself such as I have never experienced."

—*Readers' Favorite Book Review*

304 pages, 10 illustrations
978-0-9840029-5-5 (paperback), 978-0-9840029-6-2 (Mobi)
978-0-9840029-0-0 (ePub)

To purchase *Mary Magdalene Beckons*
in book, e-book, or audiobook format, please visit:

www.marymagdalenebeckons.com